THE BIRTH OF A SYSTEMIC NATION

THE AMOUNT OF MELANIN ON YOUR SKIN CAN STUNT AND HINDER YOUR GROWTH TO SUCCESS.

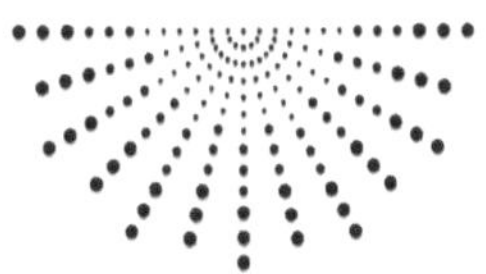

DEGOL S TEKESTE

TABLE OF CONTENTS

DEDICATION

EMMETT TILL - MEDGAR EVERS - GEORGE JUNIUS STINNEY JR. - DR MARTIN LUTHER KING JR - HENRY SMITH - JOHN CRAWFORD III - MICHAEL BROWN - EZELL FORD - DANTE PARKER - MICHELLE CUSSEAUX - MARY TURNER - LAQUAN MCDONALD - MALCOLM X-TANISHA ANDERSON - AKAI GURLEY - TAMIR RICE - RUMAIN BRISBON - JERAME REID - MATTHEW AJIBADE - JAMES N. POWELL JR. - FRANK SMART - ERNEST LACY - NATASHA MCKENNA - TONY ROBINSON - ANTHONY HILL - MYA HALL - PHILLIP WHITE - ERIC HARRIS - WALTER SCOTT - WILLIAM CHAPMAN II - ALEXIA CHRISTIAN - BRENDON GLENN - VICTOR MANUEL LAROSA - JONATHAN SANDERS - FREDDIE CARLOS GRAY JR. - JOSEPH MANN - SALVADO ELLSWOOD - SANDRA BLAND - ALBERT JOSEPH DAVIS - DARRIUS STEWART - BILLY RAY DAVIS - SAMUEL DUBOSE - MICHAEL SABBIE - BRIAN KEITH DAY - CHRISTIAN TAYLOR - TROY ROBINSON - ASSHAMS

PHAROAH MANLEY - MICHAEL STEWART - FELIX KUMI -
KEITH HARRISON MCLEOD - JUNIOR PROSPER -
LAMONTEZ JONES - PATERSON BROWN - DOMINIC
HUTCHINSON - ANTHONY ASHFORD - ALONZO SMITH -
TYREE CRAWFORD - INDIA KAGER - LAVANTE BIGGS -
MICHAEL LEE MARSHALL - JAMAR CLARK - RICHARD
PERKINS - PHILLIP PANNELL - NATHANIEL HARRIS
PICKETT - BENNI LEE TIGNOR - MIGUEL ESPINAL -
MICHAEL NOEL - KEVIN MATTHEWS - BETTIE JONES -
QUINTONIO LEGRIER - KEITH CHILDRESS JR. - JANET
WILSON - RANDY NELSON - ANTRONIE SCOTT -
WENDELL CELESTINE - DAVID JOSEPH - CALIN
ROQUEMORE - DYZHAWN PERKINS - CHRISTOPHER
DAVIS - MARCO LOUD - JAMES BYRD JR. - PETER GAINES
- TORREY ROBINSON - DARIUS ROBINSON - KEVIN
HICKS - MARY TRUXILLO - DEMARCUS SEMER -
AMADOU DIALLO - WILLIE TILLMAN - TERRILL THOMAS
- DEMETRIUS DUBOSE - ALTON STERLING - PHILANDO
CASTILE - TERENCE CRUTCHER - PAUL O'NEAL -
ALTERIA WOODS - BOBBY RUSS - JORDAN EDWARDS -
AARON BAILEY - RONELL FOSTER - STEPHON CLARK -
COREY CARTER - ANTWON ROSE II - TAYLER ROCK -
MALICE GREEN - RAMARLEY GRAHAM - ELIJAH
MCCLAIN - AIYANA STANLEY JONES - BOTHAM JEAN -
PAMELA TURNER - DOMINIQUE CLAYTON - SEAN BELL -
ATATIANA JEFFERSON - JEMEL ROBERSON - JAMES LEE
ALEXANDER - RYAN MATTHEW SMITH - DERRICK
AMBROSE JR. - ADDIE MAE COLLINS - CAROL DENISE
MCNAIR - CAROLE ROBERTSON - CYNTHIA WESLEY -
NICHOLAS HEYWARD JR. - CHRISTOPHER WHITFIELD -

WILLIE MCCOY - VICTOR WHITE III - MARCUS DEON SMITH - CHAVIS CARTER - MARTIN LEE ANDERSON - CHRISTOPHER MCCORVEY - BRADLEY BLACKSHIRE - TIMOTHY THOMAS - REGINALD DOUCET JR. - DANROY "DJ" HENRY JR. - KARVAS GAMBLE JR. - ERIC REASON - KORRYN GAINES - REKIA BOYD - KIONTE SPENCER - DARIUS TARVER - WAYNE ARNOLD JONES - MANUEL ELLIS - VICTOR DUFFY JR. - KOBE DIMOCK-HEISLER - CLINTON R. ALLEN - DONTRE HAMILTON - TIMOTHY CAUGHMAN - SYLVILLE SMITH - COREY JONES - TYRE KING - ERIC GARNER - MILES HALL - KENDRICK JOHNSON - CHARLEENA LYLES - MICHAEL LORENZO DEAN - TRAYVON MARTIN - RENISHA MCBRIDE - KIMONI DAVIS - KIWANE CARRINGTON - OSCAR GRANT III - BREONNA TAYLOR - KALIEF BROWDER - WALTER WALLACE JR. - DARRIEN HUNTWALTER - TROY HODGE - WILLIAM GREEN - AHMAUD ARBERY - DION JOHNSON-MARCELLIS STINNETTE-TONY MCDADE - ANDREW KEARSE - JAMEL FLOYD - GEORGE FLOYD - RAYSHARD BROOKS - ITALIA MARIE KELLY - DAVID MCATEE - CHRIS BEATY

ABOUT THE AUTHOR

Degol S. Tekeste is a knowledge seeker who studies Success. In his quest for financial freedom, he inspires and encourages all to seek greatness within themselves. He resides in California.

-Inspiring Greatness

PROLOGUE

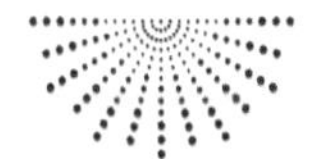

The ongoing social, economical, and political disenfranchisement of Black people in the United States cannot be overstated. Since the abolition of slavery in 1865, Black people have been, and continue to be, either in law or in practice, subject to housing discrimination, mortgage discrimination, job discrimination, educational discrimination, police brutality, and exclusion from political representation. This prejudice has resulted in the cycle of poverty, mass incarceration, worse health outcomes, and limited social mobility for Black people in the US.

WHITE MONEY

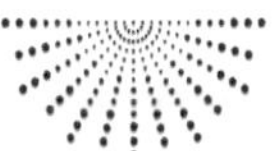

According to the Federal Reserve data, the number of White millionaires in the United States has more than doubled in the last 25 years, with 1 in 7 White families now worth more than 1 million dollars. In a 1992 survey of consumer finances, that figure was reportedly at 7 percent. This drastic growth in White millionaires reflects the continuous wealth disparity between White Americans and Black Americans. In 2016, the top 1 percent of households (mostly White Americans) held a staggering 24 percent of income, a record high in 2016. The percentage of Black and Hispanic households worth more than $1 million has remained stagnant at around 2 percent since 1992.

That's unfathomable! Especially in todays world, were minorities are the ones that drive and stir the US economy. The combined buying power of Black Americans, Asian Americans, Native Americans and Hispanic Americans, accumulates to a whooping 3.9 trillion dollars. That's a great turn out for so called "minorities".

An analysis done by the Urban Brookings Tax Policy Center, (a leading group of nonpartisan experts) reported that the Republican tax plan passed by the Trump's administration widen the country's wealth disparity resulting in major gains for the top 1 percent of Americans. In 2016, the average White American household was worth approximately $171,000. That number is now 10 times that of Black families, and 8 times that of Hispanic families.

As time passes, these numbers will only continue to increase. Why? Because White families continue to out perform Black families in several key indicators of wealth. For instance, White Americans out perform Black Americans in homeownership, equity, inheritance, and investments. White families are twice as likely to own stocks or mutual funds compared to Black and Hispanic families. According to the Federal Reserve data, 60 percent of White families invest in the stock market, while less than one-third of Black and Hispanic families have any exposure to the stock market.

This is detrimental in accumulating generational wealth in the long haul. The median value of White owned investments rose to $50,000 in 2016 while the median value of Black owned and Hispanic owned investments remained at $12,000. When it comes to homeownership, (often the largest component of wealth for American families), nearly 75 percent of White families owned their homes, compared to less than 50 percent of Black and Hispanic families. Even among homeowners, minority owned homes had lower property values. This is due to an ongoing practice called redlining (a systematic policy that prohibits minorities from purchasing property in White owned neighborhoods).

According to Valerie Wilson, (director of the Economic Policy Institute's program on race, ethnicity, and the economy) *"If you are a Black homeowner, you are more likely to have a lower value on your home because of neighborhood segregation. The average Black family can't afford to purchase properties in White communities where values are rising faster".*

Additionally, White families are more likely to trade up to pricier homes over time. In comparison, Black families are more likely to lose their homes or stay in the same house for a lifetime, said Brendan O'Flaherty, a Columbia University economist who studies the economics of race. Black and Hispanic families are also less likely to inherit wealth than their White counterparts. According to researchers, 25 percent of White households reported receiving an inheritance, compared to only 8 percent of Black households, and 5 percent of Hispanics households.

The labor market also discriminates against minorities. Studies revealed that White sounding names receive 50 percent more callbacks than ethnic sounding names. This is where the wealth gap continues to widen.

A FIELD EXPERIMENT on labor market discrimination was conducted by Professor Marianne Bertrand and Sendhil Mullaiathan. They discovered that individuals named Emily and Greg were more likely to be employed than individuals named Lakisha and Jamal.

The Experiment

Professors Mullainathan and Bertrand conducted the field experiment to examine the level of racial discrimination in the labor market by using a randomized field experiment.

Nearly 5,000 resumes were sent in response to over 1,300 newspaper ads for sales, administrative, and clerical jobs in Boston and Chicago. The resumes were randomly assigned to either a "Black sounding" name (such as Lakisha Washington or Jamal Jones) or a "White sounding" name (such as Emily Walsh or Brendan Baker) to imply the applicant's race.

These names were chosen according to a frequency data obtained from Massachusetts birth certificates from 1974 and 1979. The validity of the names "Blackness" or "Whiteness" was confirmed by surveys in public areas in Chicago. These resumes also varied by quality, with higher quality resumes listing experiences such as, summer employment, education credentials, volunteering experience, certifications aquired, special honors, and prior work experience.

The resumes were then sent out to each job opening. The responses of prospective employers were measured according to a given resume's ability to elicit a call back, or e-mail request for an interview.

The Results

The results of this field experiment indicates that, all other things being equal, race is still an important factor in the US labor market today. Resumes with White sounding names received 50 percent more callbacks than those with ethmic sounding names. The field experiment also discovered that federal contractors and employers who listed **"Equal Opportunity Employer"** in their ad discriminated as much as other employers.

Moreover, race greatly affects how much applicants benefit from having more experience and credentials. White applicants with higher quality resumes received 30 percent more callbacks than Whites with lower quality resumes. Having a higher quality resume has a smaller impact on Black applicants, who experienced only a 9 percent on callbacks.

This disparity suggests that in the current state of the labor market, Black Americans don't have strong individual incentives to build better resumes. Studies revealed that among those with no criminal records, White applicants were more than twice as likely to receive a callback relative to equally qualified Black applicants. Even more startling was that Whites applicants with a felony conviction, fared just as well, if not better, than a Black applicant with a clean background. There's no denying it, with all other things being equal, racial discrimination still exists in the US labor market today.

* * *

IN TODAYS WORLD, wealth is not just money in the bank. Wealth is reassurance against tough times. Tough times like today, where people are being laid off and forced to find other means to provide for their families. The wealth gap between the haves and have nots will continue to be relevant in the US and throughout the world if preventive measures are not taken immediately. Practices such as redlining and other forms of discriminative policies have to be eradicated in order to close the wealth gap between White and Black Americans.

2

REDLINING

edlining is one of the largest form of institutionalized racism in the US. It's a process by which banks and other institutions refuse to offer mortgages to customers in certain neighborhoods based on their racial and social economic status. The origin of the term stems from the policies developed by the Home Owners Loan Corporation (HOLC) in 1933 by the Franklin Roosevelt administration. Banks, insurance companies, loan associations, and other financial services companies used this policy. The main objective of redlining was to reduce home foreclosures during the depression era. Federal housing agencies such as the HOLC and the FHA used this policy to determine whether areas were deemed fit or unfit for investment.

The process is dubbed redlining for the presumed practice of mortgage lenders of drawing red lines around portions of a map to indicate areas or neighborhoods which were seen unfit for business. These red areas were predominantly occupied by people in certain socioeconomic groups (usually people of color and those with lower incomes).

Areas that were deemed fit for investments were outlined in green shading. Areas that were deemed still desirable were outlined in blue shading. Areas that were deemed as decline were outlines in yellow shading. The areas that were deemed as unfit, were outlined with red shading. These decisions were arbitrarily based on the area's racial composition rather than income levels.

This discriminatory pattern of disinvestment and obstructive lending practices delayed and impeded home ownership among Black communities. This policy allowed banks and other financial institutions to deny loans to Black Americans and other minorities in the US. Although redlining was formally outlawed in 1968 with the passage of the Fair Housing Act, it still persists to this very day.

History Of Housing Discrimination

Fifty years after the abolition of slavery, local governments continued to legally enforce housing segregation through exclusionary zoning laws. These exclusionary zoning laws prohibited the sale of property to Black citizens. After the Supreme Court ruled that these zoning laws were unconstitutional, homeowners replaced them with racially restrictive covenants. As a result, agreements between property owners were formed in which they banned the sale of homes to certain racial groups (usually minorities).

According to a magazine article, 80% of neighborhoods in Chicago and Los Angeles carried racially restrictive covenants by 1940. By the time the Supreme Court found racially restrictive covenants unconstitutional, the practice was so widespread that these agreements were difficult to invalidate and almost impossible to reverse.

The Federal Government And Redlining

Prior to 1934, the federal government was not involved in housing. That all changed when the Federal Housing Administration (FHA) was created as part of the New Deal. The FHA sought to restore the housing market after the Great Depression by incentivizing homeownership and introducing the mortgage lending system we still use today.

Instead of creating policies to make housing more equitable, the FHA did the opposite. It took advantage of racially restrictive covenants and insisted that the properties they insured use them. Along with the Home Owner's Loan Coalition (HOLC), a federally funded program was created to help homeowners refinance their mortgages. Due to this, the FHA introduced redlining policies in over 200 American cities.

Green, Blue, Yellow and Black Red

Beginning in 1934, the HOLC was included in the FHA underwriting handbook "residential security maps". This new policy was predominantly used to help the government decide which neighborhoods were deemed secure for investments and which were off limits for issuing mortgages.

The maps were color coded according to these guidelines:

Green ("best") areas represented in demand, up and coming neighborhoods where professional men lived. These neighborhoods were explicitly homogenous, lacking "a single foreigner or Negro." Blue (still desirable) neighborhoods had "reached their peak" but were thought to be stable due to their low risk of "infiltration" by non White groups. Yellow (definitely declining) areas bordered Black neighborhoods. They were considered risky due to the "threat of infiltration of foreign born, negro, or lower grade populations." Red (hazardous) neighborhoods where "infiltration" had already occurred. These neighborhoods, (almost all of them) were populated by Black residents. These areas were described by the HOLC as having an "undesirable population" and as a result were ineligible for FHA backing.

These maps helped the US government decide which properties were eligible for FHA backing loans. Green and blue neighborhoods, which usually had White populations, were considered good investments. It was easy to get a loan in these areas. Yellow neighborhoods were considered "risky" and red areas (those with the highest percentage of Black residents) were ineligible for FHA backing.

The Effects Of Redlining Today

The impact of redlining is still felt today. The impact goes beyond the individual families who were denied loans based on the racial composition of their neighborhoods. Numerous neighborhoods that were labeled "yellow" or "red" by the HOLC back in the 1930s are still underdeveloped and underserved compared to nearby "green" and "blue" neighborhoods with largely White populations today. Blocks in these neighborhoods tend to be empty, ran downed or lined with vacant buildings. They typically lack basic services like banking, healthcare, and have fewer job opportunities and transportation options. The neighborhoods that banks and other financial institutions deemed unfit for investment were left underdeveloped. Attempts to improve these neighborhoods with even relatively small scale business ventures were commonly obstructed by financial institutions that continued to label the neighborhoods as unfit/too risky for business.

When existing businesses collapsed, new ones were not allowed to replace them. This left entire blocks vacant. Consequently, Black Americans in these neighborhoods were frequently limited in their access to banking, healthcare, retail merchandise, and even grocery stores. One notable exception to this was, and still is, the proliferation of liquor stores and bars which seemingly transcended the area's stigma of financial risk.

Redlining also led to a shortage of employment opportunities. As a result, these neighborhoods were not seen as prospective, which scared future employers from opening new businesses. Crime often followed in the wake of these declining neighborhoods, making future investment less likely. These developments created a cycle which seemingly justified the initial redlining practices.

The government may have put an end to the redlining policies that it created in the 1930s, but as of today, it has yet to offer adequate resources to help neighborhoods recover from the damage that these policies inflicted.

Minorities And Mortgage Companies

A study by the Center for Responsible Lending, (a nonprofit research group based in North Carolina) examined 50,000 subprime loans nationwide and discovered that Black and Hispanic applicants were **30 percent more likely than White applicants to be charged higher interest rates**.

Even among borrowers with similar credit ratings, the data remained the same. In the Middle Village and Ridgewood sections of Queens, both of which have White majorities and had a median income of $47,820 in 2005, 16.7 percent of the loans were issued by subprime lenders.

In the Sheepshead Bay and Gravesend areas of Brooklyn, which mostly has White occupants, had a median income of $40,000. Yet, only 10.8 percent of the mortgages were from subprime companies. Majority of Black and Hispanic neighborhoods with median incomes of $40,000 to $50,000 had far higher rates, including East Flatbush, where 44 percent of the loans were from subprime companies, and Queens Village (34.6 percent). Therefore, Black and Latino applicants are less likely to get a mortgage, and when they do, they're more likely to pay substantially higher interest rates than their White counterparts.

Preventing Redlining

The Home Mortgage Disclosure Act was created in 1975 to help put an end to redlining and other discriminatory lending practices. The law requires lenders to track and regularly report loan level data to the Consumer Financial Protection Bureau. In return, this allows the CFPB and Department of Justice to regularly evaluate lending practices to ensure that borrowers are being treated fairly, equitably, and in line with Fair Housing practices.

For example, the CFPB may use HMDA data to see how loan pricing and interest rates compare across different ethnic groups with similar credit scores. It may also look at the underwriting standards those groups are held too.

Discriminatory Vs. Creditworthy

It's important to note the difference between discriminatory and creditworthy. While banks and lenders can't deny you a loan based on your race, gender, or disability, they can deny you for other reasons. Financial institutions have a legal and moral responsibility to deny loans to individuals who are not creditworthy and cannot repay the debt.

This may at times seem discriminatory, but approving loans for people without the means to repay them created the foundation for the Great Recession. Naturally, lenders, as well as the institutions that regulate them, want to discourage similar events from reoccurring again in the foreseeable future. Banks are free to set their own lending standards based on economic characteristics such as credit score, debt levels, and employment income.

The Fair Housing Act also allows lenders to consider things like the property's condition, local home values, neighborhood amenities, and their own need for a balanced loan portfolio when evaluating an applicant. Banks can also refuse to approve loans on properties they deem unworthy of investment. For example, if a buyer wanted to purchase a home in an area where regular flooding or landslides occurs, a bank does not have to approve the request for a mortgage. This is completely within the legal guidelines. There's no debating that. What banks and other financial institutions cannot do, is deny loans to communities/individuals due to their racial composition.

* * *

WHEN A MORTGAGE APPLICATION officer asks you for your ethnicity, it might be a good idea to answer that question truthfully. Why? Because the federal government now collects and reviews information from loan applications to determine whether redlining is still occurring. This practice not only discriminates against Black people as a whole, but it also effects young Black boys and girls across the country. According to studies, almost half of Black boys and girls live in households in the bottom fifth of the income distribution, compared to just over 1 in 10 White children. By eradicating redlining, we as a society can forever alter the lives of young Black boys and girls across the nation.

3

BORN TOO LOSE

Black and White children are born into two different social-economic status. According to researchers, almost half of Black boys and girls live in households in the bottom fifth of the income distribution, compared to just over 1 in 10 White children. Nearly half of Black youths are raised in the bottom quintile. Using data on 4,200 Black and White Americans, researchers found that 54 percent of Black men born into households in the poorest fifth of the family income distribution end up, as individuals, in the poorest fifth of the earnings distribution for their respective gender (between the ages of 28 and 35) compared to White men (22%), White women (29%), and Black women (34%). In terms of their individual earnings, Black women have similar odds of escaping poverty as White women, though both these groups lag behind the upward mobility of White men. These analyses don't consider the income of other family members. When one looks at adult family incomes, as opposed to individual earnings, a very different picture emerges for Black Americans. Black men and women have low family income mobility than White men and White Women.

According to researchers, 62 percent of Black women face a very high risk of being stuck in poverty, surpassing the 50 percent risk faced by Black men. For White Americans, the odds of remaining stuck in poverty remain relatively low, for both men (28 percent) and women (33 percent).

Among those who grew up poor, Black women are the only group showing a marked difference between the risk of being in the bottom quintile of the individual earnings distribution (for each gender), and the risk of being in the bottom quintile of the family income distribution (for the whole age cohort). White men do well on both counts, whereas Black men do poorly on both counts.

Constant Loop Of Poverty

According to studies, Black Americans born into poverty are less likely to move up the income ladder verses their White counterparts. Why? Because of the disparity of the educational inequalities, neighborhood effects, workplace discrimination, access to credit, and rates of incarceration.

Gender is also a big part of the story too, as detailed in a new paper from the Equality of Opportunity Project, "Race and Economic Opportunity in the United States: An Intergenerational Perspective" by Raj Chetty, Nathaniel Hendren, Maggie Jones, and Sonya Porter. Researchers discovered that race gaps in intergenerational mobility largely reflect the poor outcomes for Black men.

The report is another contribution to the growing literature showing that race gaps in the intergenerational persistence of poverty are in large part the result of poor outcomes for Black men. Studies also revealed that Black men born to low income parents are much more likely to end up with a low individual income than Black women, White women, and White men.

As they write: "we conclude based on the preceding analysis that the Black-White intergenerational gap in individual income is substantial for men, but quite small for women. It is important to note, that this finding does not imply that the Black-White gap in women's individual incomes will vanish with time. This is because Black women continue to have substantially lower levels of household income than White women, both because they are less likely to be married and because Black men earn less than White men."

In an attempt to estimate the impact of different marriage rates, researchers calculated the intergenerational mobility rates of Black and White men raised in both single parent and married families. They found little differences. As they concluded, "parental marital status has little impact on intergenerational gaps".

Researchers also confirmed the differences in upward earnings mobility for Black men compared to both Black women and White men. They also confirmed that Black women, despite their solid earnings mobility, have very low family income mobility. When they researched the impact of racial differences in marriage rates by simulating higher marriage rates among Black women, they found no significant effects.

Lower Marriage Rates Aren't Hurting Black Mobility

Contrary to popular belief, low marriage rates in the Black community is not hurting their upward mobility. Various explanations could be given to why lower marriage rates aren't hurting Black mobility. The most obvious one is, assuming marriages or cohabitation mostly occur within racial groups, Black women's family position is damaged directly or indirectly by the poor outcomes for Black men. If white women end up with White men, who in terms of their earnings are more than twice as likely to escape poverty as Black men, their family income will be higher.

Equally, if Black women are more likely than White women to end up as single, they will also record a lower family income. If one was to model the impact of household formation by artificially equalizing the marriage rates of Black women and White women, the results will of course depend not just on whether they marry, but also on whom they marry. While there is a drop in the rates of poverty persistence for Black women, it is a modest one (from 62 percent to 56 percent).

Support Black Men

What conclusions can be drawn from all this data? Well, for starters, the key to closing income disparities for both

Black and White women is to close intergenerational gaps in income between Black and White men. This is certainly one of the most important implications in enchasing the quality of life of both Black and White Americans. Breaking the cycle of poverty for Black Americans requires a transformation in the economic outcomes for Black men, particularly in terms of earnings. One important point here is that the relationship between earnings and marriage runs in both directions. All in all, closing the race gaps is an upward mobility and will require wholesale shifts in economic outcomes, especially in Black men's earnings.

4

SCHOOL OF HARD KNOCKS

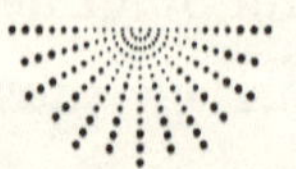

In the US, the school to prison pipeline is an ongoing problem that has received little to no media coverage. Minors and young adults, usually from disadvantaged backgrounds, are being incarcerated in masses due to harsh school and municipal policies. In recent years, the mass incarceration of Black students have grown out of control. Children as young as six years old are being detained. Incidents like theses are why the school to prison pipeline continues to persist today. For instance, the story of Isaiah Elliott, a 12 year old Black student from Colorado who was suspended for playing with his toy gun in an art class via zoom. A teacher spotted Isaiah brandishing a toy gun while playing with a friend, and notified school officials after she wasn't sure whether or not Isaiah was brandishing a toy gun or a real gun. The gun in question was a green and black plastic toy gun, with a bright orange tip and the words

Zombie Hunter printed on the side. How the teacher could've mistaken this for a real gun is incoherent.

To add fuel to the fire, deputies were sent to Isaiahs house. According to the deputies, they responded to the Eliot's residence for a "welfare" check. As one can imagine, 12 year old Isaiah was petrified. In a news interview, Isaiah explained how scared he felt when he heard the deputies knock on his door. "I didn't know what was going to happen. I didn't know if they were going to bust down the door, my heart was beating super fast." Instead of calming the young boy down with some words of encouragement and reassurance, the deputy went on to tell Isaiah "this could potentially lead to criminal charges in the future," and pressed him to pay attention to his studies. In the end, Isaiah was suspended for a duration of five days.

IN ANOTHER INCIDENT, a 14 year old Black student from Fresno, California was suspended for a haircut. According to news reports, the student came to school with a new haircut that featured a design. The school decided that his haircut violated the school code and the student was pulled out of from his classes for the remainder of the school day. His parents were informed of the incident and were told that he needed to "fix" his hair before retuning to school. When the student returned to school the next day, without "fixing" his haircut, the school informed his mother that her son would be facing an in-school suspension.

In the summer of 2018, Faith Fennidy, an 11-year-old

Black girl from Louisiana, was sent home from a private Roman Catholic school because she had hair extensions. Faith has been wearing hair extensions to school for the last 2 years with no incidents. This all changed when the school introduced a new dress code policy. This new policy prohibited students from wearing extensions and weaves to school. Luckily for Faith, her parents didn't wait around for the school to suspend or arrest their daughter. They acted promptly and withdrew their daughter from the school.

In 2018, a Black male student in Arizona wore a blue bandana to school that violated the school's dress code. Instead of finding a way to deescalate and resolve this matter, the boys teacher decided to call law enforcement. As a result, the student was not only suspended for nine days, but arrested and taken into police custody.

In 2012, a six year old Georgia student, Salecia Johnson, was crying and throwing a tantrum in her principal's office. Instead of comforting the young girl, the principal decided otherwise. He was reported saying that she, Faith, was "inconsolable, had thrown various items, and damaged school property during the tantrum". Bear in mind that this is a six year old child. As a result, Faith, a six year old Black girl, was handcuffed, arrested, and transported to the local police station.

Faith was initially charged as a juvenile with simple battery of a schoolteacher and criminal damage to property. However, the charges were later dropped after the police department decide she would not be charged due to her age.

Stories like these are rampant all over the country. Thanks to social media and parents speaking up, this phenomenal is now starting to attract media coverage. Why does this continue to happen? Well, the school to prison pipeline is the result of disproportionate disciplinary actions taken against students of color. To say it frankly, this still occurs due to racism and discrimination. There's no way around it. If the tables where turned, and all the children in these stories where White, a Disney movie would've already been shot, produced and distributed in theaters near you.

This Discipline Gap

The disciplinary policies and practices disproportionately effects Black and Latino students. This is reflected in the rates of incarceration. Between 1999 and 2007, the percentage of Black students being suspended has increased by twelve percent, while the percentage of White students being suspended has declined since the implementation of zero tolerance policies. Of the total incarcerated population in the United States, 61% are Black or Latino.

School disciplinary policies disproportionately affect Black and Latino youth than their White counter parts. In the education system, a practice known as the discipline gap, revealed that Black and Latino students are more likely to be suspended than White students. According to researchers, 5% of White students are suspended from school, compared to 16% of Black students.

Black students make up approximately 16% of the total student enrollment. Nevertheless, Black students represent 27% of students referred to law enforcement, and 31% of students subjected to all school related arrests.

All together, 70% of students involved in "In-School arrests/disciplined" are vastly Black and or Latino students. The majority of these arrests are under zero tolerance policies. As one can imagine, this discipline gap is also connected to the achievement gap.

Achievement Gaps In The United States
Racial Achievement Gap

Black students are suspended and expelled at a rate three times greater than that of White students. The advancement project discovered that "in the 2006-2007 school year, there was no state in which White students were suspended more often than Black students." This further support the claim that school to prison pipeline is effecting Black and Latino students. Disparities were found in the implementation of zero tolerance policies in relation to minor offenses. In 2010, in North Carolina Black students were punished for the same minor offenses, specifically cell phone, dress code, and disruptive behavior by more than 15 percent for each category of offense than White students.

According to the American Civil Liberties Union, zero-tolerance policies criminalize minor infractions of school rules, while cops in school lead to students being criminalized for behavior that should be handled inside the school grounds. Minorities, especially Black students, were more likely to be disciplined for less serious offenses than their White counterparts. White students were disciplined less on more serious grounds, such as possessing drugs or carrying a weapon.

Additionally, a 2010 study revealed that Black students were likely to be referred to the principals office more than White students. According to Fordham Law Review Online, "In the juvenile justice system, Black girls are the fastest growing demographic when it comes to arrest and incarceration."

In another 2015 study using a national high school dataset concluded that "misconduct and deviant attitudes were important factors in predicting the receipt of (out of school suspensions) though results indicated that Black students did not generally misbehave or endorse deviant attitudes more than White students did".

These interdisciplinary policies and practices disproportionately impact students from historically disadvantaged backgrounds such as Latino and Black students. It has also been noted that students of minority groups were vulnerable to expulsions. Additionally, Black girls are highly criminalized for being absent from a school than any other race. Schools with a higher percentage of Black students that implement this zero tolerance policies, are further implementing and supporting the school to prison pipeline effecting Black boys and girls throughout the country.

Mental Health Relating To The School To Prison Pipeline

Where there are undetected and untreated child mental health concerns, this can lead to unwanted suspensions and expulsions. When teachers include strategies to address the concerns found in students, it leads to students wanting to pursue their own academic achievement and success.

Undoubtedly, students with behavioral issues in school strongly correlates with later prison incarceration. Black students, a historically disadvantaged group, are under-diagnosed with ADHD. This systemic mislabeling leads to future difficulties with academic concentration. When these students do not receive proper treatment and diagnosis for ADHD and other mental health issues, problems can arise and leave them vulnerable to incarceration. Namely, under diagnosis of ADHD, over punishment in schools due to racist practices within schools, and over representation of minorities in the school to prison pipeline.

Positive reinforcement methods can drastically decrease classroom behavioral problems and encourage students to be more academically inclined, thus less likely to be arrested. Students react more often to positive and empathetic approaches to teaching about the dangers of crime than negative and critical ones.

BLACK LIVES MATTER: PART 1

At the start of the 2016 NFL season, San Francisco 49ers quarterback Colin Kaepernick sat on the bench while the national anthem played throughout Levi's Stadium. At first, nobody took noticed. A couple weeks later, the one time Super Bowl champion transitioned to kneeling during the National Anthem. The following week, the stand was embraced by millions of people across the country. NFL players and athletes around the league followed his lead and kneeled during the national anthem to protest police brutality. As a result, a new movement was born. It was condemned by many, including the President, who called for kneeling athletes to be kicked out of their leagues. It's been nearly five years since Kaepernick's nonviolent demonstration began. Fast forward to today and nothing has changed.

As of lately, cities across the US have been rocked by protests against police brutality following the May 25 killing of an unarmed Black Minneapolis man named George Floyd by a White officer. This has now resulted in a nationwide protests demanding an end to police brutality towards Black Americans.

According to Vox, an estimated 45 million Americans have adopted more progressive views on race and racism since protests began in 2014. While public opinion has changed, policing outcomes in most places have not. Racial disparities such as arrests and deadly force continue to persist. As cell phone cameras continue to capture police brutality and violence towards unarmed Black citizens, tension seem more insurmountable than ever.

Police Brutality And The African American Community

In the US alone, Black Americans are 2.5 times more likely to be killed by police than White Americans. For Black women, the rate is 1.4 times more likely. In fact, people of color in general were found more likely to be killed by police than their White counterparts. That's according to a new study conducted by Frank Edwards, of Rutgers University's School of Criminal Justice, Hedwig Lee, of Washington University in St. Louis's Department of Sociology, and Michael Esposito, of the University of Michigan's Institute for Social Research.

The researchers used verified data on police killings from 2013 to 2018 compiled by the website Fatal Encounters, created by Nevada based journalist D. Brian Burghart. Under their models, they found that roughly 1 in 1,000 Black boys and men will be killed by police in their lifetime. For White boys and men, the rate is 39 out of 100,000.

Cases Where Unarmed Black Citizens Where Brutally Murdered By Law Enforcement

In March 2018, police officers in Sacramento, California, fired at least 20 bullets at 22-year-old Stephon Clark, killing him. He was unarmed and running away. Three months later, a Pittsburgh police officer killed 17-year-old Antwon Rose, shooting him in the back. He was unarmed and fleeing.

Five months later, a Hoover, Alabama, police officer killed 22-year-old Emantic Bradford Jr. He was shot three times, all from behind. That year alone, law enforcement killed a total of 1,165 people. In fact, there were only 22 days in all of 2018 where police didn't kill someone.

Despite all the protests, marches, training seminars, thoughts and prayers, in 2018 alone, cops killed 36 more people than they did the year before, according to Mapping Police Violence and the Washington Post. Despite being 12.6 percent of the US population, Black people were 26.7 percent of the people killed by police where the race was known. The number of Black people killed by police in 2018 (215) was more than all the police who died in the line of duty (148), US servicemen killed in action (2) and Americans killed by Islamic terrorists (0) combined.

Startling Statistics Of Unarmed Citizens Killed By Law Enforcement

In 2018, Black people were three times more likely to be killed by police than their White counterparts. 28 percent of the unarmed victims of police killings were Black and only 48 percent were White. 34.9 percent of the people killed by cops, even though they were unarmed and not attacking, were Black. 113 individuals were shot and killed by police officers as they were fleeing the scene on foot. 35 percent of the individuals killed were Black. Although non-Hispanic Whites make up 62 percent of the population, most of the unarmed, armed, and fleeing victims killed by police in 2018 were people of color.

There was no category of police shootings where police killed more White people. If that doesn't have your blood boiling, this will. A staggering 90 percent of the officers involved in the 1,165 police killings in 2018 were not charged with a crime! Not a single one! "No justice, no peace."

The Death Of George Floyd: An Unarmed Black Man Killed In Police Custody

On May 25, 2020, George Floyd, a 46-year-old unarmed Black man, died in Minneapolis, Minnesota, after Derek Chauvin, a White police officer, knelt on his neck for almost nine minutes while he was handcuffed face down in the street. Two other officers further restrained Floyd and a fourth officer prevented onlookers from intervening.

During the final three minutes Floyd was motionless and had no pulse. Officers made no attempt to revive him, and Chauvin's knee remained on his neck as emergency medical technicians attempted to treat him. Floyd had been reportedly arrested on suspicion of passing a counterfeit $20 bill at a nearby convenience store (Cup Foods market).

Several witnesses took videos of the incident, which were

widely circulated and broadcast along with security-camera footage from nearby businesses. In the now viral video footage, one can clearly see that Floyd was face down on the ground with three officers applying pressure to the back of his neck, torso and legs.

A criminal complaint later filed against Chauvin stated that Floyd repeatedly said he could not breathe while standing outside a police car, resisted getting in the car, and intentionally fell down. "He went to the ground face down and, after Chauvin placed his knee on Floyd's neck, Floyd repeatedly said "I can't breathe", "Mama", and "please".

Two autopsies determined the manner of Floyd's death to be ruled a homicide. All four officers were fired the day after the incident, and criminal charges were brought against them. Chauvin was charged with second degree murder and second-degree manslaughter. The other three are charged with aiding and abetting second degree murder.

After Floyd's death, demonstrations and protests against use of excessive force by police officers and lack of police accountability were held globally. Protests in the Minneapolis–Saint Paul had turned violent as a police precinct and two stores were burned, and many stores were looted. As a result, Floyd's death triggered major protests in Minneapolis, and sparked rage across the entire country.

Racial Disparities In Police Violence

One of the key reason of Kaepernick's protest was to shed light on the fact that Black Americans were more likely to be killed by law enforcement than white Americans. Those officers who were responsible of the deaths of Black Americans were not being held accountable of their actions.

Black Americans account for about 12.5% of the overall US population but accounted for more than 22% of those killed by police. White Americans account for nearly two-thirds of the population but made up less than half (42.3%) of those killed by police.

In a country with 18,000 law enforcement agencies, each with different issues and outcomes, changing these outcomes on a nationwide scale requires sustained organizing and advocacy efforts in every jurisdiction. To do this, communities need the tools to effectively evaluate each law enforcement agency and hold them accountable to measurable results.

How To Stop Police Brutality

There are substantially different perspectives about what police should or should not do. These differences cannot all be resolved at once, but there are a preventive measures that can be adopted by law enforcements all over the country to evaluate any police department responsibility for protecting people from harm. For example, law enforcement around the country should prioritize protecting people from violence and limiting arresting people for low level offenses.

Furthermore, law enforcement tent should avoid the use of brute force, especially deadly force, to the greatest extent possible. In addition, when people come forward to report misconduct by employees of the agency, it should result in some form of accountability and preventative measures should be taken immediately.

Lastly, when people call on the police to help solve crimes, if the encounter results in a death, citizens should be able to trust that department to find the officer responsible guilty, if sufficient evidence is presented. The department should accomplish these goals in ways that are not biased or discriminatory in any way, shape, and form. And only then will we start to see a shift of justice moving forward.

Generational Policing

Police Brutality has been an issue in our country for centuries. It's one of the biggest problems we have in America today. Over the last 30 years, at both the national and local levels, governments continue to dramatically increased their spending on criminalization, policing, and mass incarceration while drastically cutting investments in basic infrastructure and slowing investment in social safety programs.

No one is arguing or stating that being a police officer is an easy job. Matter of fact, being an officer is one of the most stressful and dangerous career path one can pursue in life. With that being said, it's a risk they've chosen to assume, and no matter what, it's unreasonable to argue that simply choosing to take that risk means that an officer should never be held accountable for taking the life of a person they swore an oath to serve and protect.

As analysis and data show, civilians are increasingly dying at the hands of police officers at an alarming rate. With Black Americans, Pacific Islanders, Hispanics and Native Americans being more likely than white Americans to be victims of police injustice despite being in the minority.

As the rate at which officers are charged with crimes has fallen by 90%, and the charge to conviction rate is nearly non existence. In this day and age of civilization, Black Americans should not be murdered and brutalized by law enforcement with near impunity. Until these matters are resolved, Black Lives Matters will continue to protest the injustice at the hands of law enforcement.

6

BLACK LIVES MATTER: PART 2

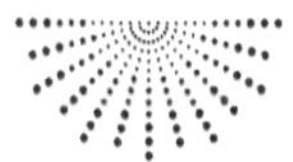

The deaths of George Floyd, Travon Martin, Tamir Rice, Sandra Bland, Ahmad Arbery, Breonna Taylor and hundreds of other innocent Black citizens who've lost their lives due to police brutality, has shed some light on an ongoing issue referred to as systematic racism. According to the FBI Uniform Crime Reporting program and the Bureau of Justice Statistics National Prisoners Statistics program, studies reveled that Black Americans are nearly three times as likely to be incarcerated than their White counterparts. Studies revealed that Black Americans were twice as likely to be arrested than White Americans. Furthermore, as a minority in the US, Black Americans have an incarceration rate more than five times higher than that of White Americans. In other words, if you are Black, you can expect to be arrested in the foreseeable future.

While some may argue and repute this claim, one can't

ignore the facts. Data collected on the subject matter indicates that there is irrefutable data and evidence backing this claim.

There is a funnel of unequal justice where Black Americans are more likely to be arrested and more likely to be incarcerated than White Americans. This is a fact, not an opinion. Several key findings support and validate that a racial disparities in incarceration exists in modern day America.

The biggest discrepancy is among Black men. Black men are six times more likely to be incarcerated than White men. The largest racial discrepancy is among young Black men. 18 to 19 year old Black Americans are over 12 times to be incarcerated while 20 to 24 year old Black Americans are eight times more likely to be incarcerated.

If The Tables Were Flipped

If Black Americans were incarcerated at the same rate as White Americans, there would be over 294,000 fewer Black Americans in prisons. To put this figure in perspective, that is more than the number of fans that can fit in the 15 largest NBA arenas (the average stadium capacity is 18,966). If you do the math correctly, that tallies up to 284,490 Black lives that would be free if they were melanin deficient.

Conversely, if White Americans were incarcerated at the same rate as Black Americans, there would be nearly an additional three quarters of a million incarcerated White Americans (739,362). This is equivalent to the number of fans that would fit in 10 NFL stadiums (an average seating capacity of a NFL stadium is 69,444). Let that sink in for a moment.

When the tables are turned, one can clearly see the disparity between Black and White Americans being incarcerated in the US.

Even though Black people account for 13% of the national population, they make up a staggering 33% of the prison population. And in 2018, nearly a half million (465,200) Black Americans were incarcerated in the US. If thats not shocking enough, according to studies, Black Americans who are arrested are three times more likely to end up in federal or state prison than their White counterparts.

Using FBI arrests data, Black Americans have a 22% likelihood of being imprisoned while White Americans have a 8% likelihood of being incarcerated. In other words, more than 1 in 5 African Americans who are arrested are likely to end up in prison, compared to 1 in 12 White Americans. That's preposterous, especially in todays world, where equality is plastered on every corner.

If you carefully look at the statistics, you'll see the coalition between mass incarceration in the Black community. The economic repercussions of mass incarceration of the Black community is visible to the naked eye, yet nothing significant is being done by city officials to resolve this generational exile of Black people.

The discrepancy in racial likelihood to be incarcerated cannot be explained by severity or type of crime alone. Focusing on just male prisoners, research by the United States Sentencing Commission discovered that Black offenders receive longer prison sentences than their White counterparts.

For instance, the White Duke University student that

raped a women and got away Scott free on probation because the judge thought that he had a bright future ahead and it would be a shame to throw it all way. In a similar case, a Black person was arrested for a similar crime and sentenced to 30 years in prison. This is just one of numerous cases where judges hand down the hammer on Black people simply because Black people are perceived as a threat to society.

Incarceration Statistics

- Black American are over twice as likely to be arrested after a police-initiated interaction than White Americans.
- While 29% of White Americans are arrested after police-initiated interactions, 60% of Black Americans are arrested.
- If Black Americans were arrested at the rate of White Americans, over 1.1 million fewer Black Americans would be arrested each year; they could fill all 29 NBA stadiums, twice.
- If White Americans were arrested at the Black rate, over 5.7 million more White Americans would be arrested (this is equivalent to the population of Colorado).
- Police are twice as likely to threaten or use force on Black Americans than White Americans (this includes the threat and actual use of force such as grabbing, pushing, hitting, kicking, handcuffing, pepper spray, Taser, or pointing of a gun).

- A Black American is threatened with or experiences use of force by police every 3 minutes.
- 1 in 58 Black households is likely to have at least one person be threatened with or personally experience use of force in America each year.
- Police are nearly three times more likely to fatally shoot a Black American than White American.
- In 2018, 229 Black Americans were killed by the police; to put this figure in perspective, a Black person is killed by police every 38 hours.
- Black Americans are over twice as likely to be arrested, over twice as likely to be threatened or experience use of force, and nearly three times more likely to be killed by police.

Racial Disparities In Mass Incarceration

Today, the US makes up about 5% of the world's population. Yet, the US makes up of 21% of the world's prisoners. According to NAACP, minorities composed of 56% of all incarcerated people in 2015 even though African Americans and Hispanics make up approximately 32% of the US population. The US imprisons a larger percentage of its Black population than South Africa did at the height of apartheid.

Add implicit biases and "War on Drugs" with structural disadvantages and your result will be a system of mass incarceration that disproportionately effects people of color.

The system in place was never designed with minorities in mind. Left unchecked, this system can marginalize populations of people and create unwarranted racial disparities. All throughout American history, Black Americans and other minority groups have been stigmatized and labeled as "dangerous," "aggressive," "super predators," "violent," and "criminals."

Researchers discovered that Black people are given harsher sentences because they pose a greater threat to public safety than White people. These implicit biases in our criminal justice decision makers are reflected in the disparities we see in sentencing and arrest rates of minorities all over the country.

According to the Bureau of Justice, since 1978, there has been a 500% increase in America's prison population. This increase is explained by sentencing law and policy, not crime rates. In noncapital cases, race is often found to contribute to disparities in sentencing, but most often in combination with variables such as gender and employment. Black and Hispanic offenders sentenced in State and Federal courts face significantly greater odds of incarceration than similarly situated White offenders.

In some jurisdictions, minorities may receive longer sentences or differential benefits from guideline departures than their White counterparts.

In the 1970s, there was an American initiative to crackdown on the drug trade and drug use, and the policies created to support this campaign is known as the "War on Drugs". Despite the conspiracies, the War on Drugs was theoretically race neutral. Yet, it had substantial racial effects.

"For drug crimes, disparities are especially severe. This is largely due to the fact that Black people are four times as likely as White people to be arrested for drug offenses and two and a half times as likely to be arrested for drug possession. Black people constituted 21% of drug arrests in 1980. That figure drastically increased to 36% in 1992 before declining to 34% by 2009, but still disproportionate to their White counterparts in all aspects".

These effects show and validate that disparities in the criminal justice system still persists till this very day. The system has failed to protect minorities from bias policing. It's evident that all three branches of government (legislative, executive and judicial) have failed to protect people of color. From initial contact with the police, to harsher policies, systematic racism effect minorities of all backgrounds.

Colorblindness

In the age of colorblindness, people like to swear that they don't see color and that victims of racial injustice are just "playing the race card". Another common remark for those defending our criminal justice system is that, people of color are more involved in crime than their White counterparts. This a false narrative that has been repeated time and time again. In spite of that, recent national media attention of police brutality has helped bring mass incarceration and police brutality towards Black citizens into the publics attention once again. The fact that 60 percent of America's prison population are comprised of minorities, despite knowing that Whites make up 60% of the population, shows that our nation's criminal justice system is rigid.

The continuous cycle of systemic disadvantages, the failed

War on Drugs, and the unconscious biases in the criminal justice system, have all contributed to the destruction of the lives of millions of Black Americans and their families.

7

BAD BLOOD: THE TUSKEGEE EXPERIMENT

As the fight over reforms to the American health-care system continues to linger, one can't help but recall the grim milestone in the history of health care in the US. Over the course of 40 years, a government medical experiment was conducted in Tuskegee, Alabama that left hundreds of Black men with syphilis to go untreated in order for scientists to further study the side effects of syphilis. Out of 600 Black men who originally took part in the study, 200 or so were left to endure the disease and its side effects without treatment, even after penicillin was discovered as a cure for syphilis. By the time the report came out, seven men involved had died of syphilis and more than 150 died of heart failure. 74 participants were still alive, but the government health officials who started the study had already retired. Because of the study's length and the way treatment options had evolved in the intervening years, it was hard to pin the blame on an individual, though easy to see that it was wrong.

The Experiment

In 1932, 600 African American men from Macon County, Alabama were enlisted to partake in a scientific experiment on syphilis. In what would become known as the infamous 40-year Tuskegee Study. The goal was to observe untreated syphilis in black populations. The subjects were unaware of the experiment and were told instead that the treatments they were receiving were for "bad blood". Many did not receive any treatment at all.

Starting in 1932, 600 African American men from Macon County, Alabama were enlisted to partake in a scientific experiment on syphilis. The "Tuskegee Study of Untreated Syphilis in the Negro Male," was conducted by the United States Public Health Service (USPHS) and involved blood tests, x-rays, spinal taps and autopsies of the subjects.

The goal was to "observe the natural history of untreated syphilis" in Black populations. The subjects were unaware of this and were simply told they were receiving treatment for "bad blood". In reality, they received no treatment at all. Even after penicillin was discovered as a safe and reliable cure for syphilis.

To really understand the heinous nature of the Tuskegee Experiment requires some societal context, a lot of history, and a realization of just how many times government agencies were given a chance to stop this human experimentation but failed to do so. In 1865, the ratification of the Thirteenth Amendment of the US constitution formally ended the enslavement of Black Americans. But by the early 20th century, the cultural and medical landscape of the US was still built upon racist concepts.

Social Darwinism was rising, predicated on the survival of the fittest, and "scientific racism" (a pseudoscientific practice of using science to reinforce racial biases) was common. Numerous White people already thought themselves to be superior to Black people, and science/medicine was all too happy to reinforce this hierarchy.

Before the end of slavery, scientific racism was used to justify the African slave trade. Scientists argued that African men were uniquely fit for enslavement due to their physical strength and simple minds. They argued that slaves possessed primitive nervous systems and didn't experience pain as White people did.

Enslaved African Americans in the South were claimed to suffer from mental illness at rates lower than their free Northern counterparts (thereby proving that enslavement was good for them), and slaves who ran away were said to be suffering from their own mental illness known as drapetomania.

DURING AND AFTER the American Civil War, African Americans were argued to be a different species from White Americans, and mixed-race children were presumed prone too many medical issues. Doctors of the time testified that the emancipation of slaves had caused the "mental, moral and physical deterioration of the Black population," observing that "virtually free of disease as slaves, they were now over-whelmed by it."

Many believed that the African Americans were doomed to extinction, and arguments were made about their physiology being unsuited for the colder climates of America (thus they should be returned to Africa).

Scientific and medical authorities of the late 19th/early 20th centuries held extremely harmful pseudoscientific ideas specifically about the sex drives and genitals off African Americans. It was widely believed that, while the brains of African Americans were under-evolved, their genitals were over-developed. Black men were seen to have an intrinsic perversion for White women, and all African Americans were seen as inherently immoral, with insatiable sexual appetites.

This all matters because it was with these understandings of race, sexuality and health that researchers undertook the Tuskegee study. They believed, largely due to their fundamentally flawed scientific understandings of race, that Black people were extremely prone to sexually transmitted infections such as syphilis. Low birth rates and high miscarriage rates were universally blamed on STIs.

They also believed that all Black people, regardless of their education, background, economic or personal situations, could not be persuaded to get treatment for syphilis. Thus, the USPHS could justify the Tuskegee study, calling it a "study in nature" rather than an experiment, meant to simply observe the natural progression of syphilis within a community that wouldn't seek treatment.

The USPHS set their study in Macon County due to estimates that 35% of its population was infected with syphilis. In

1932, the initial patients between the ages of 25 and 60 were recruited under the guise of receiving free medical care for "bad blood," a colloquial term encompassing anemia, syphilis, fatigue and other conditions. Participants were told that the treatment would last only six months. Throughout the study, participants received physical examinations, x-rays, spinal taps, and when they died, autopsies.

Researchers faced a lack of participants due to fears that the physical examinations were actually for the purpose of recruiting them to the military. To alleviate these fears, doctors began examining women and children as well. Men diagnosed with syphilis who were of the appropriate age were recruited for the study, while others received proper treatments for their syphilis (at the time these were commonly mercury or arsenic containing medicines).

In 1933, researchers decided to continue the study long term. They recruited 200+ control patients who did not have syphilis (simply switching them to the syphilis-positive group if at any time they developed it). They also began giving all patients ineffective medicines (ointments or capsules with too small doses of neoarsphenamine or mercury) to further their belief that they were being treated.

As time progressed, patients began to stop attending their appointments. To greater incentivize them to remain a part of the study, the USPHS hired a nurse named Eunice Rivers to drive them to and from their appointments, provide them with hot meals and deliver their medicines. In an effort to ensure the autopsies of their test subjects, the researchers also began covering patient's funeral expenses.

Multiple times throughout the experiment researchers

actively worked to ensure that their subjects did not receive treatment for syphilis. In 1934 they provided doctors in Macon County with lists of their subjects and asked them not to treat them. In 1940 they did the same with the Alabama Health Department. In 1941 many of the men were drafted and had their syphilis uncovered by the entrance medical exam. Upon the discovery, researchers had the men removed from the army, rather than let their syphilis be treated.

* * *

IT WAS in these moments that the Tuskegee study's true nature became clear. Rather than simply observing and documenting the natural progression of syphilis in the community as had been planned, the researchers intervened: first by telling the participants that they were being treated (a lie), and then again by preventing their participants from seeking treatment that could save their lives. Thus, the original basis for the study that the people of Macon County would likely not seek treatment and thus could be observed as their syphilis progressed became a self-fulfilling prophecy.

The Henderson Act was passed in 1943, requiring tests and treatments for venereal diseases to be publicly funded, and by 1947, penicillin had become the standard treatment for syphilis, prompting the USPHS to open several Rapid Treatment Centers specifically to treat syphilis with penicillin. All the while they were actively preventing 399 Black men from receiving the same treatments.

By 1952, about 30% of the participants had received penicillin despite the researchers efforts. Regardless, the USPHS argued that their participants wouldn't seek penicillin or stick to the prescribed treatment plans. They claimed that their participants, all Black men, were too "stoic" to visit a doctor. In essence, these men thought they were already being treated, so why would they seek further treatment?

The researchers tune changed again as time went on. In 1965, they argued that it was too late to give the subjects penicillin, as their syphilis had progressed too far for the drug to help. While a convenient justification for their continuation of the study, penicillin is (and was) recommended for all stages of syphilis and could have stopped the disease's progression in the patients.

In 1947 the Nuremberg code was written, and in 1964 the World Health Organization published their Declaration of Helsinki. Both aimed to protect humans from experimentation, but despite this, the Centers for Disease Control (which had taken over from the USPHS in controlling the study) actively decided to continue the study as late as 1969.

* * *

IT WASN'T UNTIL A WHISTLEBLOWER, Peter Buxtun, leaked information about the study to the *New York Times* and the paper published it on the front page on November 16th, 1972, that the Tuskegee study finally came to an end. At the time, only 74 of the test subjects were still alive. 128 patients had died of syphilis or its complications, 40 of their wives had been infected, and 19 of their children had acquired congenital syphilis.

There was mass public outrage, and the National Association for the Advancement of Colored People launched a class action lawsuit against the USPHS. It settled the suit two years later for 10 million dollars and agreed to pay the medical treatments of all surviving participants and infected family members, the last of whom died in 2009.

Largely in response to the Tuskegee study, Congress passed the National Research Act in 1974, and the Office for Human Research Protections was established within the USPHS. Obtaining informed consent from all study participants became required for all research on humans, with this process overseen by Institutional Review Boards (IRBs) within academia and hospitals.

The Tuskegee study has had lasting effects on America. It's estimated that the life expectancy of Black men fell by up to 1.4 years when the study's details came too light. Many also blame the study for impacting the willingness of Black individuals to willingly participate in medical research today.

* * *

WE KNOW all about Nazis who experimented on prisoners. We condemned the scientists in Auschwitz who carried out these tests on innocent people. But one cannot forget that America has also used its own people as lab rats. Yet to this day, no one has been prosecuted for their role in the Tuskegee experiment, which left 399 Black men to endure the effects of syphilis. As a result of the Tuskegee experiment, Black Americans have developed a lingering, deep mistrust of public health officials that persists to this very day.

8

BLACKS FOR SALE

*C*ivilizations in the past have be known to use slave labors to build their fortresses. However, what transpired in Africa was and is considered one of the largest slave trading in human history. The Trans-Atlantic slave trade was unique in size, geographic reach and global significancc. From the first slave ship departing Africa in 1525, (to the Americas) to the last (to Cuba) in 1866, more than 12 million Africans were loaded on to the Atlantic slave ships. The 11 million plus that managed to survive such horrible conditions, were scattered across the Americas. Majority of them destined for the tropical and semi-tropical economies of Europe's colonial powers. Once there, enslaved Africans were used in every major industry from extracting precious metals and timber, growing and harvesting coffee, building railways, to cultivating tobacco, rice and sugar. There was never a shortage of labour for these industries among the Europeans.

Before 1820, more Africans landed in the Americas than

Europeans. In the Americas, the enslaved Africans were the critical pioneers of laying sown the basis for a thriving "New World" which later lured millions of migrants from Europe.

On their explorations of the African coast in the 15th century, Europe's maritime, led by the Portuguese, found sources of gold and of slave labour, both bought and exchanged from African traders. Their initial trade in slaves developed between different African societies. Luckily, a hostile environment, and especially disease, prevented Europeans (with a few notable exceptions) to establish civilization in Africa.

Meanwhile, in America, Europeans were in need of labour due to the vast decline of the Native Indian population. As a result, Europeans need of slave labour in Africa came together into a profitable trade, with slaves transported in large numbers across the Atlantic. The slave ships concentrated on African societies familiar with slavery (in the form of women, prisoners of war or criminals).

How The Trans-Atlantic Slave Trade Transpired

The trans-Atlantic slave trade was the largest long-distance forced movement of people in recorded history. From the sixteenth to the late nineteenth centuries, over twelve million (some estimates run as high as fifteen million) African men, women, and children were enslaved, transported to the Americas, and bought and sold primarily by European and Euro-American slaveholders as property used for their labor and skills.

The trans-Atlantic slave trade occurred within a broader

system of trade between west and Central Africa, Western Europe, and north and south America. In African ports, European traders exchanged metals, cloth, beads, guns, and ammunition for captive Africans brought to the coast from the African interior, primarily by African traders.

Many captives died during the long journeys to the coast. European traders then held the enslaved Africans who survived in fortified slave castles such as Elmina in the central region (now Ghana), Goree Island (now in present day Senegal), and Bunce Island (now in present day Sierra Leone), before forcing them into ships for the Middle Passage across the Atlantic Ocean.

Historians estimate that 10 to 19 percent of the millions of Africans forced into the Middle Passage across the Atlantic died due to rough conditions on slave ships. Those who arrived at various ports in the Americas were then sold in public auctions or smaller trading venues to plantation owners, merchants, small farmers, prosperous tradesmen, and other slave traders.

These traders could then transport slaves many miles further to sell on other Caribbean Island or into the North or South American interior. Predominantly European slave-holders purchased enslaved Africans to provide labor that included domestic service and artisanal trades. The majority of slaves provided agricultural labor and skills to produce plantation cash crops for national and international markets. Slaveholders used profits from these exports to expand their landholdings and purchase more enslaved Africans, perpetuating the trans-Atlantic slave trade cycle for centuries to come.

Establishing The Trade

In the fifteenth century, Portugal became the first European nation to take significant part in African slave trading. The Portuguese primarily acquired slaves for labor on Atlantic African Island plantations, and later for plantations in Brazil and the Caribbean. They also sent a small number to Europe.

Initially, Portuguese explorers attempted to acquire African labor through direct raids along the coast, but they found that these attacks were costly and often ineffective against west and Central African military strategies.

For example, in 1444, Portuguese marauders arrived in Senegal ready to assault and capture Africans using armor, swords, and deep sea vessels. Upon arrival, the Portuguese quickly discovered that the Senegalese out-maneuvered their ships using light and shallow water vessels that were better suited in the Senegalese coast.

Additionally, the Senegalese out smarted the Europeans with their unique battle skills. Unlike the Europeans, the Senegalese fought with poison arrows that slipped through their armor and decimated the Portuguese soldiers.

Subsequently, Portuguese traders generally abandoned direct combat and established commercial relations with west and Central African leaders, who agreed to sell slaves taken from various African wars or domestic trading, as well as gold and other commodities, in exchange for European and North African goods.

Over time, the Portuguese developed additional slave trade partnerships with African leaders along the West and

Central African coast and claimed a monopoly over these relationships, which limited access to the trade for other western European competitors. Despite Portuguese claims, African leaders enforced their own local laws and customs in negotiating trade relations. Many welcomed additional trade with Europeans from other nations.

When Portuguese, and later their European competitors, found that peaceful commercial relations alone did not generate enough enslaved Africans to fill the growing demands of the trans-Atlantic slave trade, they formed military alliances with certain African groups against their enemies. This encouraged more extensive warfare to produce captives for trading. While European backed Africans had their own political or economic reasons for fighting with other African enemies, the end result for Europeans traders in these military alliances was greater access to enslaved war captives.

To a lesser extent, Europeans also pursued African colonization to secure access to slaves and other goods. For instance, the Portuguese colonized portions of Angola in 1571 with the help of military alliances from Kongo, but were pushed out in 1591 by their former allies. Throughout this early period, African leaders and European competitors ultimately prevented these attempts at African colonization from becoming as extensive as in the Americas.

The Portuguese dominated the early trans-Atlantic slave trade on the African coast in the sixteenth century. As a result, other European nations first gained access to enslaved Africans during wars with the Portuguese, rather than through direct trade. When English, Dutch, or French privateers captured Portuguese ships during Atlantic maritime conflicts, they often found enslaved Africans on these ships, as well as Atlantic trade goods, and they sent these captives to work in their own colonies.

In this way, privateering generated a market interest in the Trans-Atlantic slave trade across European colonies in the Americas. After Portugal temporarily united with Spain in 1580, the Spanish broke up the Portuguese slave trade monopoly by offering direct slave trading contracts to other European merchants.

Known as the *Asiento* system, the Dutch took advantage of these contracts to compete with the Portuguese and Spanish for direct access to African slave trading, and the British and French eventually followed. By the eighteenth century, when the trans-Atlantic slave trade reached its trafficking peak, the British (followed by the French and Portuguese) had become the largest carriers of enslaved Africans across the Atlantic. The overwhelming majority of enslaved Africans were transported to plantations in Brazil and the Caribbean, and a smaller percentage went to North America and other parts of South and Central America.

The Trade

The transatlantic slave trade is sometimes known as the Triangular Trade, since it was three-sided, involving voyages; from Europe to Africa, from Africa to the Americas, and lastly from the Americas back to Europe. It's generally seen as a 'trade' since it revolved around transactions, or a form of exchange, between the African sellers and the European buyers of captives. Indeed, it would have been impossible for European slave traders to venture into Africa and procure African captives without some African involvement. African kingdoms and societies were too strong and well organized. Even when Europeans built forts on the coast of West Africa, this was on land given, or rented, from Africans for this purpose.

Racism

Another legacy of the slave trade is the continued existence of a body of ideas initially formulated to justify it and which now underpins modern anti-African racism in all its forms. These harmful ideas have no basis in fact but were and are designed to suggest that Africa and Africans are inferior to Europe and Europeans in a variety of ways.

These views permeated the centuries of the slave trade and the enslavement of Africans and continued to be expressed during the post-slavery colonial era. They still exist today in the form of racial stereotypes and prejudices and racist violence, as well as Eurocentric views about Africa, its peoples and their cultures.

The End Of The Slave Trade

At the time of the American Revolution (1775–83), there was widespread support in the northern American colonies for prohibiting the importation of more slaves. After the revolution, at the insistence of Southern states, Congress waited more than two decades before making the importation of slaves illegal. When Congress did so, in 1808, the law was enacted with little dissent, but Caribbean smugglers frequently violated the law until it was enforced by the Northern blockade of the South in 1861 during the American Civil War. After Great Britain outlawed slavery throughout its empire in 1833, the British navy diligently opposed the slave trade in the Atlantic and used its ships to try to prevent slave-trading operations. Brazil outlawed the slave trade in 1850, but the smuggling of new slaves into Brazil did not end entirely until the country finally enacted emancipation in 1888.

The slave trade finally came to an end due to a variety of factors, including the protests of millions of ordinary people in Europe and the United States. Its abolition was also brought about by millions of Africans who continually resisted enslavement and rebelled against slavery in order to be free. Resistance started in Africa, continued during the so-called Middle Passage and broke out again throughout the Americas. The most significant of all these acts of resistance and self-liberation was the revolution in the French colony of St. Domingue, now Haiti, in 1791. It remains the only successful slave revolution in history and led to the creation of the first modern black republic. Haiti's constitution was the first to recognize the human rights of all its citizens.

First Denmark in 1803, and Britain in 1807, and then other countries in Europe and the Americas abolished the transatlantic slave trade for a variety of reasons including changes in their economic requirements. Nevertheless, an illegal trade continued for many years, and slavery itself was not abolished in some countries until the 1880s. In Brazil for example, slavery continued to be legal until 1888.

The Atlantic crossing remains perhaps the best-known passage for slaves, but there were other enormous slave routes that scattered Africans and their descendants across great distances. Over the course of a millennium, Africans were forcibly marched across the Sahara to the slave markets of north Africa.

Other routes saw captives moved eastwards, to the slave markets off east Africa, and then to Arabia and to India. Meanwhile, for those crossing the Atlantic, landfall did not bring an end to their enforced travels. After landing, they were moved onwards, to inland settlements and properties. Some Africans were relocated and transported to the North American backcountry, to remote plantations in Caribbean valleys and mountains, and deep into the vastness of South America, even high into the mining districts of the Andes.

Slaves in the Americas could never feel secure. They would be uprooted and moved again and again. Some were re-sold, inherited, relocated with the movement of owners, and or through the misfortunes of economic upheaval or warfare. After 1800, the US cotton industry drew slave labour south and west from the old slave states. Almost a million people were uprooted in this way. One slave family in five was wrecked in the process, and one slave child in three was torn from their parents.

At the same time, an internal slave trade in Brazil was even larger. Forcibly moving people from old regions too newly opened industries (notably coffee). Long after the Atlantic slave trade had ended, the buying and selling off humans continued to affect the lives of millions. Even after various European countries and new American nations officially ceased their participation in the slave trade, illegal trans-Atlantic slave trading persisted even after national and colonial governments issued legal bans.

The international slave trade had long lasting effects on the African landscape. Areas that were hit hardest by endemic warfare and slave raids suffered from general population decline, and it is believed that the shortage of men in particular may have changed the structure of many societies by thrusting women into roles previously occupied by their husbands and brothers. Additionally, some scholars have argued that images stemming from this era of constant violence have survived to the present day.

Finally, the increased exchange with Europeans and the vast wealth it brought enabled many states to cultivate sophisticated artistic traditions employing expensive and luxurious materials.

When slavery finally ended in America after nearly three centuries, much of the wealth generated by the transatlantic slave trade supported the creation of industries and institutions in modern North America and Europe today. To an equal degree, profits from slave trading and slave-generated products funded the creation of fine art, decorative arts, and architecture that continues to inform aesthetics today. From the fine silver and gold work of Dahomey and the Asante court, to the virtuoso wood carving of the Chokwe chiefdoms. These treasures are a vivid testimony of the turbulent period in African history.

The Impact Of Slavery On Black Progress

In order to address the impact of slavery in today's society, it is important to address why slavery happened in the first place. Among the most common arguments in support of slavery in the colonial era include the fact that it was a way of life and it led to the economic development of most world powers. Individuals who defend the act look at it as something that was inevitable, where it was used to provide the much needed labor for economic development.

While this may have some truth on the surface of it, the underlying reason for slavery has everything to do with superiority. Slavery was not just started because of the need for economic development. Rather, it was a vice that was tamed from the need for superiority, where the white race saw a vulnerable people and decided to exploit them. Hence, one can infer that racism was an integral aspect of slavery.

Racism, which was the subconscious reason for slavery, is still very much alive in today's society. It's a direct repercussion of the need for one race to become superior to another. Slavery bore the seeds for racism in the society today. It provides a sense of entitlement for individuals belonging to a superior race and created an inferiority complex among those people who belonged to a marginalized race.

The lines that were drawn between Black and White begun in the days of slavery, where generations grew up with the notion that this is the manner in which the two races are supposed to co-exist. The same explains why Black people have to fight for their freedom and rights through powerful movements such as B.L.M. The White superiority ideology was already created and gave one race a powerful position over the other, which is still being showcased in today's society.

Most people would like to believe that racism ended when slavery was abolished. The reality is that racism, which is a direct result of slavery, is still rampant today. It is showcased through racial profiling, the lack of equity when it comes to the distribution of resources, and schools that still showcase segregation. Take, for instance, the case of Tyre King, a 13-year-old Black kid who was shot by the police when he reached for his BB gun.

The police assumed he was armed and dangerous because of his skin color, when in fact he was just a harmless young man. The shooting brought an outrage in the public over what many termed as police profiling. Protesters opined that a young Black children cannot walk in the neighborhood with a particular dress code or with their hands in their hood pockets because they are assumed to be armed. The protests brought back days when young Black children feared the streets because they could not walk without being gunned down by the police.

Unfortunately, the case of Tyre King is not the only one that has been in the limelight recently. There are similar shootings of unarmed Black teenagers such as Michael Brown in the media, a situation that has sparked a Black lives matter campaign and raised questions about racism. In most of these cases, the conclusion has always been that the police would not have shot the young men had they been White and reached into the pockets of their hoods to retrieve a toy gun. The situation thus sheds light on the racism that is still apparent in the society today, where Blacks are still regarded in the very stereotypes that come with being inferior to White superiority.

Impact Of Slavery On Society Today

Slavery had a direct impact on the classism system that is still very apparent in the society today. Slavery brought about the ill-treatment of African Americans that was manifested in a society that is divided into classes. The system still exist today in all facets of life, where it is felt in the political, social, and economic demographics.

In the argument about reparations, proponents posit that slavery lessened any chance that African Americans had off being competitive. They have to work twice as hard to be at the same level with their White counterparts because opportunities are not available to everyone in the society today. For this reason, African Americans still account for most of the poverty in the United States, given that the unemployment percentage among them stands at 13%.

African Americans and other minorities are at the bottom of the income percentile while their White counterparts remain at the middle-class and upper level. The rationale is that opportunities have always belonged to the superior race from the days of slavery. Even after slavery was abolished, it proved difficult to find a balance in which African Americans would still get the opportunities afforded to the former, and the same struggle is still present today. Take, for instance, the education sector. Segregation is believed to be something of the past that was abolished in the decision in Brown vs.

Education Board. However, as Lauren Camera says, "but not only do students of color and poor students often lack equal opportunities, segregation, it turns out, is still alive and well".

The segregation is experienced in the fact that poor schools, which are often dominated by African American students, lack the resources that would enable effective learning. There are still schools that have a 75% population of Black students and others with a population of 90% White, mainly private schools that have vast opportunities for students. Research indicated that Blacks and Hispanic students are dominant in poverty-stricken schools that seem to be forsaken by their districts. Such raises issues about the impact of racism and slavery, which brought about this need for classism that is still alive today.

Had American been founded on better principles, equality would have prevailed. However, slavery brought about the ideals that one race has to be superior over another, which thus brought about the current disparities being experienced by African Americans and minorities as well. Even though recent years have seen the rise in the number of African Americans who hold powerful position and are well off financially, the same can be traced to their personal efforts as opposed to what the system created for them. Most of African American idols are singers, actors, and sportsmen. Such aspects appear to be among the few avenues individuals in this cohort can excel, as opposed to their White counterparts who have a sense of entitlement that was created by the vice of slavery.

Harry S. Truman once said, there's nothing new in the world, except the history you do not know. Slavery and its effects are still being felt today through acts of racism and the classism that exist in today's society. Even as the world become more prosperous, there is no denying that modern slavery is a concern, and it is one that has its foundations on the roots society built centuries ago.

9

BLACK WALLSTREET

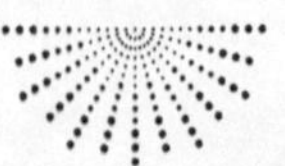

lack Wall Street was once a thriving Black owned district in Tulsa, Oklahoma. As much as it could be, it was also a safe haven for Black people escaping discrimination and oppression in the deep south. Nevertheless, in that era, White extremist couldn't allow for such a provident community to thrive. In their eyes, Black people where merely property. As a result of the mass migrations to the area, driven in part by increased job opportunities, Tulsa became the city with the most African-Americans in the state. With a boom in the Black population and their demands for equality, perceptions of discrimination and shared experience among African-American allowed for little time for adaptation among Whites.

As part of the Jim Crow south, Tulsa was highly segregated. Black voters were suppressed, tortured and lynched by White mobs. In 1921, White rioters burned down Black wall street. In their path of distraction, they killed as many as 300

Black Tulsans, left thousands homeless, and ransacked an entire neighborhood.

At the time, there were no prosecutions of the instigators. Today, almost a century later, there have been no reparations given to those that were effected by the riots.

This Is What Happened, And Why It Still Matters Today: The Rise and Fall Of Black Wall Street

In the turn of the 20th Century, Tulsa began to flourish thanks to a huge oil boom in Oklahoma. The area also saw a major uprise in Black settlers around that time. Land in Oklahoma was readily available for all. As a result of this boom, a wealthy African-American land owner, named O.W. Gurley, relocated to Tulsa In 1906 and purchased 40 acres of land. Gurley himself was born in Arkansas to former slaves and was mostly self educated. Knowing that he had zero chances of achieving success in the Jim Crow-era south, Gurley left Arkansas in the 1890s to join thousands of other homesteaders claiming land (which previously belonged to Native Americans but was made available by the federal government to westward traveling settlers).

Gurley initially settled 80 miles west of Tulsa, where he claimed the plot of land that he and other Black entrepreneurs named Greenwood.

Gurley, who witnessed discrimination and racism, had a vision to create something for Black people by Black people.

The land he purchased, was only sold to black settlers. By doing this, Gurley helped and gave Black settlers an opportunity to build and start their own businesses. In essence,

Whites were resentful that Blacks no longer passively accepted second-class citizenship in their own homeland.

Since it was against the law back then for Black people to shop at white owned stores, Black people were forced to create their own business, and as a result, their businesses flourished and prospered.

According to historians, this new community dubbed "Black Wall Street," was self contained and self-sufficient neighbored ran and operated by Black residents. Residents in this community owned and operated their own grocery stores, banks, libraries, hotels, movie theaters, etc.

At the time, Greenwood was seen as a place to escape, economic, social, and political oppression in the Deep South. It was an economy and community born out of necessity due to the Jim Crow era.

Gurley also loaned money to other black entrepreneurs looking to start their own businesses. This was important in establishing the Greenwood District as a center of Black business and wealth, as Black entrepreneurs would have otherwise had little to no opportunity to borrow money from White owned banks during the Jim Crow Era.

Gurley, a man way ahead of his time, provided an opportunity for those migrating from the harsh oppression of Mississippi. He gave Black settlers hope and prosperity. At that time, the average income of Black families in the area exceeded what minimum wage is today. As a result of segregation, a dollar circulated 36 to 100 times and remained in Greenwood almost a year before leaving. Even more impressive, at that time, was that the state of Oklahoma had only two airports, yet six Black families owned their own planes.

Years later, In 1921, Tulsa, Oklahoma's Greenwood District, known as Black Wall Street, became one of the most prosperous African American communities in the United States. But on May 31 of that year, the Tulsa Tribune reported that a Black man, Dick Rowland, attempted to rape a white woman, Sarah Page. The events that followed next, resulted in the turmoil and downfall of Black Wall Street.

Less fortunate White neighbors resented their upper-class lifestyle. As a result of a jealous desire "to put progressive, high achieving African-Americans in their place," a wave of domestic white terrorism caused Black dispossession.

False Accusation of Sexual Assault Leads To The End of Black Wall Street

In 1921, Tulsa, Oklahoma's Greenwood District, known as Black Wall Street, was one of the most prosperous African-American communities in the United States. But on May 31 of that year, the Tulsa Tribune reported that a Black man, Dick Rowland, attempted to rape a White woman, Sarah Page. White residents in the area refused to wait for the investigation to play out, sparking two days of unprecedented racial violence. 35 city blocks went up in flames, 300 people died, and 800 were injured.

Accounts vary on what happened between Page and Rowland in the elevator of the Drexel Building. Yet, as a result of the Tulsa Tribune's racially inflammatory report, black and white armed mobs arrived at the courthouse armed and ready for war. Numerous fights broke out, as shots starting ringing. Since Black people were outnumbered, they retreated and headed back to Greenwood. The enraged White mob preceded to give chase and started looting and burning down businesses and homes along the way.

Eyewitnesses at the scene claimed "the area was bombed with kerosene and/or nitroglycerin," causing the inferno to rage more aggressively. Official accounts state that private planes "were on reconnaissance missions, they were surveying the area to see what happened."

The police force also contributed to the riot. Due to their ineffective leadership, they allowed mobs to gather at the courthouse for hours before seeking additional assistance. Furthermore, they actively participated in the riot by deputizing Whites without discretion, arming them with guns to multiply the police force overnight. Meanwhile, no White people were ever arrested during the riots.

Additionally, crooked politicians and the media falsely framed the Tulsa riot as an uprising started by lawless Blacks. Tulsa newspapers regularly referred to the Greenwood district as "Little Africa" and "nigger town."

African-Americans in the district were labeled "bad niggers" who drank booze, smoked dope, and ran around with guns. Perhaps as a result of government officials stereotyping rhetoric and the media's biased reporting, Whites and Blacks interpreted the racial violence differently.

Generally, White politicians and residents perceived the Black community "as predisposed to crime and in need of social control. In other words, due to assumptions of Black criminality, Whites justified deadly violence on Black Wall Street, because Blacks needed to be subjugated.

The Tulsa World newspaper further inflamed and instigated the tensions between Blacks and Whites by suggesting that the Ku Klux Klan could "restore order in the community." Since the K.K.K asserted white superiority with terroristic acts, such as lynchings, the mere suggestion from a mainstream newspaper that the K.K.K should intervene demonstrates how White supremacy was not only legitimized but also promoted with legal impunity.

In the early 1900s, there was a rise in Black Nationalist organizations that refused to cower in the face of K.K.K violence or submit to societal subordination. Whites responded to Black pride and demands for equality with "social control, including segregation, lynchings, and pogroms".

The media framed the riot, igniting tensions. In essence, Blacks' desire for socioeconomic progress and assertion of their rights was seen as a grave threat to White supremacy. Portraying all Blacks as criminals served the Black inferiority narrative, maintained Jim Crow segregation, and promoted the violent enforcement of racist ideology.

The massacre of Black Wall Street primarily occurred due to Whites "generalized perception that African-Americans were 'out of line'" and needed to be put "back in their place." Despite all of the economic damage, neither the survivors nor their families ever received reparations.

In The End

Despite racial discrimination and Jim Crow segregation, the Greenwood district offered proof that Black entrepreneurs were capable of creating vast wealth. There is evidence that Whites perceived African-Americans as an economic threat to the city. For those who supported Black oppression, witnessing the Black community thrive and defy the stereotypes of Black inferiority was too much to bare.

Soon after the riot, Walter F. White of the National Association for the Advancement of Colored People (NAACP) visited Tulsa. According to him, Black economic prosperity contributed to the destruction of the Greenwood District. He stated that the town had grown from a population of 18,182 in 1910 too somewhere "between 90,000 to 100,000" residents by 1920. White settlers claimed that the sudden wealth of the townspeople rivaled the "forty-niners" in California.

The destruction of this successful African-American community was no accident. The destruction of the community was rationalized as a necessary and natural response to put them "back in their place".

By the end of the 1950s, more than half of the businesses had closed. Desegregation allowed the entry of businesses owned by Whites, while increasing numbers of African Americans in the community invested in entities outside Greenwood. By 1961, 90 percent of African American income in Tulsa was spent outside of the Greenwood district.

In essence, African-Americans posed a "geographical problem because their community was situated in an ideal location for business expansion." The government and private industry worked in concert to bring down land prices and maintain White dominance in the Tulsa area. Poor Whites' resentment of successful, landowning Blacks allowed elite Whites to use them as pawns to obtain more land, wealth, and prosperity. Judging by the legal impunity granted to Whites by law enforcement, the state endorsed and, in fact, supported the Tulsa riot for self-serving, capitalistic gains.

Historically, American capitalism thrived with an elite few maintaining power and wealth. When Blacks gain a strong foothold in a community or industry, they gained the power to effect meaningful change. Thus, the socioeconomic progress of African-Americans on Black Wall Street threatened the power structure of White-dominated American capitalism. When White people destroyed Black business establishments and homes, the façade of White superiority was maintained.

By the 1940s, the Greenwood District was rebuilt, but due to integration during the Civil Rights era, never regained as much prominence as it once had. The fate of Black Wall Street illustrates that as long as power remains in the hands of the elite, mainly White families, America's socioeconomic system can be marshaled to support and advance the tenets of white supremacy. Regardless of the progress made by prominent African-Americans, American capitalism is structured to keep a White people of society ahead of the remaining races.

* * *

FAST FORWARD TO TODAY, Andrew young (a civil Rights Legend) along with Killer Mike and Ryan glove, are set to open the Nation's newest Black owned bank, Greenwood Bank in homage to Black Wall Street. The bank will be the first digital bank for Black and Latinx business owners/consumers. In the end, the history of Black Wall Street and the massacre that occurred there, much like the Juneteenth holiday, and other historical black stories, continue to be nonexistence in history books. Matter of fact, as of today, these stories have yet to be addressed or included in school curriculums. As time passes, those who don't learn history are destine to repeat it.

10

BERNARD GARRETT AND JOE MORRIS

The story of Bernard Garrett and Joe Morris, two black entrepreneurs who strived to achieve the American dream in the Jim crow era, is one of the most gut wrenching example of the power of the human will. During the 1950s and 1960s, the civil rights movement dominated the country. Garrett and Morris didn't allow these circumstances to dictate their futures. Together, they set out to achieve the American dream by any means necessary. With dedication and persistence, the two visionaries beat the odds and became two of the most influential Black businessman in the Jim crow era. Without the support of banks, Black Americans were denied the opportunities to create and attain their own wealth. During those times, there was great effort to keep black people from becoming a viable economic competitor. As we all know, the building blocks to success, to building wealth, to financial freedom, is acquiring equity.

In order to create wealth, you need ownership. That's why

is so important for one to own equity such as real estate. But in those times, black people were seen as second class citizens. There were only a hand full of establishments for black people compared to their white counterparts. This ultimately hindered and impeded Black people from creating their own wealth. In the South, Black people were not even allowed access into certain buildings. The only time they were allowed asses to financial established such as banks, was if they were hired help (janitors or chauffeurs).

For Morris and Garnett, failure was not an option. In their quest to financial freedom, the duo secured bank loans for black business owners across the country.

As part of their plan, they secured a loan from a wealthy White banker to purchase real estate throughout the country. Due to being Black in that era, the duo encountered numerous obstacles and hardships. For instance, they could not present themselves publicly as owners of the buildings they acquired, preside on the board of directors, or even enter the premises unless they presented themselves as janitors or chauffeurs.

They devised a plan and set out to become two of the wealthiest Black business men in the Jim Crow era. In order to enter and survey the buildings they were trying to buy, they decided to wear disguises. They pretended to be chauffeurs and janitors. They also hired "faces," (White men that they coached to carry out their business deals) while the duo remained anonymous.

The "faces" pretended to be the CEO, overseeing the day to day operations, while Garrett and Morris, the true owners, posed as chauffeurs and janitors to monitor their ventures under the radar, either by mopping the floors of their businesses or acting as chauffeurs.

In the coming years, unbeknownst to many, the duo ended up purchasing a total 77 buildings, including what was considered to be the tallest structure in downtown Los Angeles in 1961 (the Banker's Building) all the while creating life changing opportunities for black Americans along the way.

Coming from great success, the duo strived to create opportunities for other black business men like themselves. They decided to put their lives on the line in order to help oppressed businessmen in the South. They were visionaries who set out to forever change the way the world operates today.

They continue to land bigger deals, and vouched to seek capital where capital was not available for black business owners. They wanted to create opportunities for Black Americans who were routinely subjected to redlining and other discriminative practices where banks denied colored people loans, relegating them to segregated and impoverished neighborhoods and limiting income potential in the Black community. Their end goal was to give opportunity to local black businessmen who were having difficulties obtaining business loans for their businesses.

In the coming years, their banks became a lifeline for the black community. Black owned banks were able to help African Americans to participate in the economy in ways they were never able to participate in the past.

They were now able to purchase homes, take out a small business loans to purchase appliances, cars and properties. As a result, numerous black churches and schools were helped and saved because of their banks.

* * *

In 1954, Garrett net worth was estimated to be $1.5 million dollars (equivalent to $14.3 million in todays value) making him one of the wealthiest business man in the country. Unfortunately for the duo, bank examiners claimed that Garrett and Morris were misapplying bank funds and signing off on loans that were "non-conforming". As a result, they were sued by the Federal Deposit Insurance Corporation for fraud and arrested and indicted on charges of fraud in El Paso, Texas when their business partner gave them up for a reduced prison sentence.

RICH IN GOLD & MELANIN

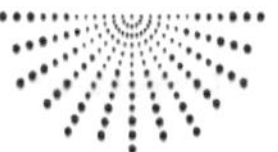

If you were to conduct a survey by asking random strangers, "what continent did the wealthiest person to ever live reside from? Africa is probably the last thing you would expect to hear as an answer. If one was to look back in history, he/she would discover that the wealthiest person to ever live was from the continent of Africa. In todays world, given the socio-economic status of most Black Americans nowadays, it can be shocking for one to believe that the wealthiest man in history was once a Black man from Africa. A Black man rich in gold and in melanin. His name was Mansa Musa, the tenth emperor of the Malian empire, (a West African territory). He was not only the wealthiest man in Mali but the wealthiest man in history. His wealth was so vast that if it was calculated and accounted for inflation, it would've doubled that of Elon Musk net worth (rich person in the world today, approximately worth 208 Billion US dollars). Thats' a staggering 400 billion US dollars in todays figures.

To put things in perspective, imagine a single individual having so much wealth, that he single handily controlled and ruled an entire region's economy for decades. In today's world, when we think of rich people, we think of names such as Jeff Bezos, Bill Gates and Elon Musk. Yet, even with their outrageous wealth, these individuals don't even come close to control the economy like the way Mansu Musa once did.

Fast forward to today, to all the turmoil and craziness, it's shocking to imagine that the wealthiest man that ever lived was estimated to have been worth double Elon Musk's current net worth. It's even harder to believe that he was from Africa. A continent synonymous with "hunger and poverty".

Who Was Mansa Musa?

Mansa Musa was the tenth emperor of the Malian empire during the thirteenth century. As one can imagine, technology in those days were pretty much non existence. As a result, the details of Mansa Musa and how he led his life are limited. Luckily, historians were able to preserve and compose a thorough background of Mansu Musa due to the preserved writings and illustrations left behind by ancient Arab scholars.

Some of the irrefutable evidence includes facts about his status as a wealthy emperor. As a self made mogul, Mansu Musa raise to power was anything but ordinary. When Abubakari Keita II, the emperor of Mali decided to embark on a quest to explore the depths off the Atlantic ocean, he appointed Musa as his interim deputy until his return. Unfortunately for Keita II, his pilgrimage to the Atlantic ocean cost him his life. As a result, Mansu Musa was appointed as the new emperor of Mali. The rest was history.

Musa took advantage of this opportunity and in return transformed Mali into one of the wealthiest regions in the world. Being strategically located, the Mali empire was rich in natural resources such as salt and gold. In return, he revamped Timbuktu, (a city in the Mali empire) into a bustling trade center that remains lucrative till this very day.

Musa was also able to extend the Mali empire into other regions. The region's wealth meant that most territories willingly joined the empire, resulting in the improvement of the people's standard of living. In other words, everyone ate under Musa's rule.

When territories refused to join the Mali empire, Musa retreated to his massive and well equipped army that could easily defeat any other African territory at the time. In his reign of approximately 25 years, Musa never lost a battle in his life. As a result, Musa grew his Mali empire to a larger region. To put this in perspective, if Musa was still emperor today, his empire would've included modern day Senegal, Mauritania, Niger, Côte d'Ivoire, Guinea, Guinea-Bissau, Burkina Faso and Gambia.

Although the Mali empire was extremely rich and vast, this was not a well known fact since travel was limited in those days. Few outsiders witnessed the extent of Musas empire and wealth. Luckily, things changed when Musa decided to embark on a pilferage to Mecca.

Mansa Musa's Pilgrimage To Mecca

In spite of the danger ahead, Musa and his followers decided to embark on a quest to Mecca. As a devout Muslim, he took it upon himself to make that long and treacherous pilgrimage to the mecca. On his pilgrimage, he took with him an entourage of 60,000 men. All those who traveled with Musa were dressed lavishly and were well fed throughout the Pilgrimage. At the time, this move by Musa was unprecedented. No other empire could afforded to do the same.

On his Pilgrimage to Mecca, Musa traveled through Cairo, where he showered people with gold. By doing this, Musa made a name of himself. His acts of generosity got the town people talking and as a result, news of Musa's wealth spread far and wide. Along his way, Musa gave the poor gold to enhance their standard of living. As generous as this may have been, the influx of gold in Cairo led to price increases which threatened to crash the entire economy.

Upon realizing this, on his way back to his empire from Mecca, Musa borrowed back all the gold he could retrieve by paying a high-interest rate. By doing this, he was able to stabilize the Egyptian economy. This shows and highlights Musaas knowledge and power. The man single handedly controlled an entire economy. Not too many people can do that today.

The End Of Musas Empire

Like every other story, theres a begging a middle and an end. After a quarter century as an Emperor, Musa finally succumbed to his death in 1337 at the age of 57. He was the link that kept the Mali empire intact and in power. Once his children took over as rulers, the empire slowly but gradually began to break off. As word got out about the vast wealth in Mali, numerous European nations began to invade the region. In the following years, the Mali empire eventually succumbed to French colonial rule.

All in all, Musa was not only the richest man in history, but a great philanthropist and leader. Under his rule, he enhanced and positively altered the lives of millions of Africans. Historians credit him with driving education within the continent. He staffed the University of Sankore in Timbuktu with world class astronomers, jurists, and mathematicians. Till this very day, the university remains one of the top universities in Africa.

Although Musa's legacy and story is not known taught worldwide, he remains an influential figure in West Africa. This is the type of stories young Black Americans should be taught in school. Stories like Mansa Musas should be all over the history books. Sadly, stories like this are buried and never brought up due to the lack of relevancy it has on White America. In other words, history is written by those it favors.

CELEBRATING BLACK EXCELLENCE

*B*lack history shaped, and continues to shape the world we live in today. For most of United States history, African American experience and culture developed outside of mainstream America. Black history, in the forms of African culture, slavery, and the civil rights movements, shaped, and continues to shape, the African American experience through religious practices, familial and community systems, political position, and economic behaviors.

Additionally, legal and social discrimination denied African Americans access to education and literacy. Institutionalized discrimination combined with African and slave traditions contributed to the retention and cultivation of a cultural tradition that survives to this day in the African American experience. This way, the tradition that permeated Black history continues to enrich the religious, political, and business worlds of the African American experience and continues to transform mainstream American culture and experience.

Years of institutionalized discrimination and the civil rights movement that brought its demise, are hugely important elements of Black history. The wake of the non violent civil rights movement produced the Black Arts Movement. This movement birthed the rise of music and literature that reflected and embraced a pronounced political and racial consciousness.

In many ways, the 1960s and 1970s was a period of Black history where African Americans made major strides toward equality while simultaneously embracing their unique African and American heritage. In doing so, the African American experience is shaped by rich, cultural, economical, political, and religious movements and people that refused to be minimized by the larger mainstream culture.

Just recently, we as a nation, began to finally recognize and celebrate the accomplishments, achievements, and contributions of African Americans in all our myriad shades, and shapes. African Americans are part of a long, proud, profound, and difficult history of the building of the United States and have contributed to all parts of American society.

As we recognize the significance of the African American experience and culture, we also fully acknowledge that the participation, engagement, and partnership of African Americans in this history is a moment by moment endeavor of hearing the voices that built this country.

Some of America's most amazing innovations have come from Black people. To get a sense of why that might be, it's important to understand the history of what we now call the

United States Of America from the perspective of the Black experience.

In the year 1619, approximately twenty Africans were kidnapped from their villages near what is known today as Angola and arrived in the state of Virginia. The current year, 2021, marks the 402nd anniversary of the first time slaves arrived in what we know today as the United States.

For over two centuries, Africans were kidnapped from their homeland, forced on ships where 250–600 of them were chained in the cargo area, and sold across Europe and throughout the Americas. Once these humans were purchased, they were bred to primarily perform manual labor where they suffered physical abuse.

The US Constitution originally considered African Americans 3/5 of a citizen. Later, the 13th Amendment abolished slavery, the 14th Amendment granted former slaves full citizenship, and the 15th Amendment granted Black Men the right to vote. Soon after, African Americans were considered "separate but equal". Forced segregation also meant that African Americans could not attend the same schools, eat at the same diners, and drink from the same water fountains as White Americans.

This history is important to keep in mind for two primary reasons. First, Black people were and continue to be innovative, creative, and brilliant, even after enduring the constant oppression. And, it is important because this oppression has led to a lack of awareness of innovation, creativity, and brilliance, in the Black community.

Secondly, all too frequently when we think of Black History month, the spotlight focuses only on the most high profile figures such as Martin Luther King Jr., Malcolm X, Jackie Robinson, Rosa Parks, and their roles in the civil rights movement. Harriet Tubman acting as the "conductor" of the Underground Railroad, and Jackie Robinson becoming the first Black person to end segregation in baseball.

It's not that Martin Luther KingJr., Harriet Tubman and Malcom X and Jackie Robinson aren't important, it's just that there numerous other African Americans who have played a key role in US history and have yet to have their contributions recognized.

In this chapter, we will cover and celebrate the history of Black people who have made an impact in shaping our world today.

Black Excellence

Gerald A. Lawson (1940-2011): Anyone who owns a Sony Playstation, Nintendo Switch, or Xbox should know Lawson's name. He created the first home video game system that used interchangeable cartridges, offering gamers a chance to play a variety of games. This approach also gave video game makers a way to earn profits by selling individual games, a business model that exists today. Lawson, who died in 2011 at age 70, was just beginning to be recognized by the gaming industry for his pioneering work prior to his death.

Garrett Morgan (1877-1963): After witnessing an accident between a horse-drawn carriage and an automobile, Morgan had an idea. His three-position traffic signal, patented in 1923, helped save lives at a time when cars, horses, and pedestrians all shared the road. But this wasn't even his most famous invention. Morgan received a patent in 1912 for his safety hood and smoke protector (a precursor to today's gas mask). His forward thinking led to saving the lives of countless people across the globe.

Marc Hannah (1956-): Anyone amazed by the special effects showcased in modern day movies should thank Hannah. The computer scientist is one of the founders, in 1982, of the software firm Silicon Graphics (now SGI), where the special-effects genius developed 3-D graphics technology that would be used in many Hollywood movies. Donkey Kong fans also owe a debt of gratitude to Hannah as he was instrumental in designing the Nintendo 64 gaming system.

Valerie Thomas (1943-): In an era when girls weren't even encouraged to study math and science (a problem that still persists in the US today), Thomas eagerly sought information about technology. She would eventually earn a degree in physics and land a job at NASA in the mid-1960s, where she would work into the 1990s. In 1980 she received a patent for the illusion transmitter, an early form of 3-D technology. Uses for the technology have yet to be fully realized, but with the increased interest in 3-D, her work will surely be an integral part of the future.

Mark Dean (1957-): Dean is one of technology's top innovators. This computer engineer helped design the IBM personal computer, introduced in 1981, that became a staple on desktops. He, along with co-inventor and IBM colleague Dennis Moeller, helped develop the interior hardware that would allow computers to connect to various peripherals, such as printers and monitors. Ironically, the man who helped make the PC popular is now using only tablets, noting in a blog post, "When I helped design the PC, I didn't think I'd live long enough to witness its decline."

Shirley A. Jackson (946-): Jackson is known for her innovative work in theoretical physics and semiconductor theory. In 1995, US President Bill Clinton appointed the physicist chairwoman of the US Nuclear Regulatory Commission, making her the first woman and first African American to hold this prestigious position. In 2002, Discover Magazine named her one of the 50 Most Important Women in Science.

Bessie Coleman (1892-1926): Coleman was the first black woman to fly an airplane. When American flying schools denied her entrance due to her race, she taught herself French and moved to France, earning her license from Caudron Brother's School in just seven months. She specialized in stunt flying and performing aerial tricks. Reading stories of World War I pilots sparked her interest in aviation.

Claudette Colvin (1939-): Colvin was arrested at the age of 15 for refusing to give up her seat to a white woman, nine months before Rosa Parks more famous protest. Because of her age, the NAACP chose not to use her case to challenge segregation laws. Despite a number of personal challenges, Colvin became one of the four plaintiffs in the Browder v. Gayle case. The decision in the 1956 case ruled that Montgomery's segregated bus system was unconstitutional.

Mary Fields (1832–1914): Known as "Stagecoach Mary," Fields was the first African-American to work for the US postal service. Born a slave, she was freed when slavery was outlawed in 1865. At age 63, Fields was hired as a mail carrier because she was the fastest applicant to hitch a team of six horses. She never missed a day, and her reliability earned her the nickname "Stagecoach". If the snow was too deep for her horses, Fields delivered the mail on snowshoes, carrying the sacks on her shoulders.

Harriet Jacobs (1813 – 1897): Born a slave, her mother died when she was 6. She moved in with her late mother's slave owner who taught her to sew and read. In 1842 she got a chance to escape to Philadelphia, aided by activists of the Philadelphia Vigilance Committee. She took it and worked as a nanny in New York. Her former owners hunted for her until her freedom was finally bought in 1852. She secretly began to write an autobiography which was published in the US in 1860 and England in 1861. She lived the rest of her life as an abolitionist, dedicated to helping escaped slaves and eventually freedmen.

Nelson Mandela (1918 – 2013): Mandela spent most of his life campaigning for an end to apartheid in South Africa. After over 20 years in prison, he was released and was able to be the first elected President in post-apartheid, South Africa. He was also admired for his forgiveness and willingness to reach out to the white community in South Africa.

Barack Obama (1961-): In 2008, Obama became the first US President of African origin. Obama served two terms as President and was awarded the Nobel Peace Prize. Obama implemented health care reform and spoke about the need for Americans to remain united, despite differences of political opinion.

Jesse Owens (1913-1980): Won four Olympic Golds at 'Hitler's Olympics', Berlin 1936. Owens maintained a dignified stance on civil rights, despite enduring discrimination during his life.

Desmond Tutu (1931 –): Leading figurehead in the South African anti-apartheid movement. Desmond Tutu is also a leading figure in speaking out for humanitarian and civil rights issues.

Mohammed Ali (1942 – 2016): Great boxer of the 1960s. Refused to fight in Vietnam. Then a controversial decision, he later became widely admired as a principled figure of great stature.

Frederick Douglass (1818-1895): A former slave, Douglass became a leading figurehead in the anti-slavery movement. One of the most prominent African American leaders of the Nineteenth Century. His autobiography of life as a slave, and his speeches denouncing slavery — were influential in changing public opinion.

Kofi Annan (1938 –): UN Secretary-General from Ghana who served two terms. Widely admired for his skills of patience and diplomacy.

Toussaint Louverture (1743 – 1803): Leader of Haitian slave revolt. In 1791, he led the successful military revolt in Saint-Domingue and over the next years consolidated his power and influence restoring the plantation system with paid labour. Louverture enabled the colony to end slavery and in 1804 declared itself the independent Republic of Haiti.

Booker T. Washington (1856 – 1915): Author and orator, Washington was an adviser to the presidents of Roosevelt and Taft. During the late nineteenth and early twentieth century, he was often considered the *de facto* leader of African-Americans. He advocated an incremental approach to improving education and life prospects of black Americans.

W.E.B. Du Bois (1868 – 1963): Du Bois was an influential

African-American activist who sought to campaign for full equality between blacks and whites. He rejected the Atlanta compromise of 1909 but insisted on full equality. Thought little change was achieved in the 'Progressive Era,' Du Bois laid the framework for the NAACP and future civil rights movements.

Pele (1940 –): Pele was the greatest footballer of the century. Since retirement, Pele become a global ambassador for sport and is a well-known advocate of overcoming poverty.

Oliver Tambo (1917 – 1993): President of the ANC (1960 – 1990). Tambo was a leading figure in promoting international opposition to the apartheid regime in South Africa.

Michael Jordan (1963 –): Considered the greatest basketball player of all time. He was six times NBA champion and played an influential role in popularizing basketball in 1980s and 1990s.

Thurgood Marshall (1908 – 1993): US civil rights lawyer and the first African-American appointed to the US Supreme Court Justice. Marshall was the lead lawyer in the pivotal Supreme Court Case *Brown vs Board of Education, Topeka* (1954) which overturned legal segregation in the US.

Chinua Achebe (1930 – 2013): Best selling Nigerian novelist. He wrote the 1958 classic, *'Things Fall Apart'* Achebe was interested in religion and the influences of both Christianity and native African traditions. Professor at Bard College, the US.

Usain Bolt (1986 –): Usain Bolt is an iconic figure in athletics. He won triple Olympic gold at the 2008, 2012 and

2016 Olympics, and broke the world record for 100 m and 200 m. Also took part in sport with a natural enthusiasm and joy.

Carl Lewis (1961 –): Nine-time Olympic gold medalist, Carl Lewis won gold over three Olympics and was the great star of 1980s track and field.

Bob Marley (1945 – 1981): Jamaican singer-songwriter. Cultural legend and global music star. A committed Rastafari who helped make reggae an international phenomenon.

Sojourner Truth (1797 – 1883): African-American abolitionist and women's rights campaigner. In 1851, gave a famous extemporaneous speech "Ain't I a woman?" which supported equal rights for blacks and women.

Ida Wells (1862 – 1931): Wells was a pioneering journalist and newspaper editor. She used her position to investigate the practice of lynching in the South. A fearless civil rights activist and female suffrage campaigner, she was a founder member of the NAACP in 1909.

Hattie McDaniel (1895 – 1952): McDaniel was an actress, comedian, and singer-songwriter. She was the first African-American actress to be awarded an Oscar for best-supporting actress in the 1939 film "Gone With the Wind"

Abiy Ahmed (1976–): Is an Ethiopian politician serving as 4th Prime Minister of the Federal Democratic Republic of Ethiopia. He was the third chairman of the ruling Ethiopian People's Revolutionary Democratic Front from the Oromo Democratic Party (ODP), which was one of the four coalition parties of the EPRDF. Abiy was also awarded the 2019 Nobel Peace Prize for his work in ending the 20-year post-war territorial stalemate between Ethiopia and Eritrea.

Billie Holiday (1915–1959): American jazz singer. Given the title "First Lady of the Blues." Billie Holiday was widely considered to be the greatest and most expressive jazz singer of all time. Her voice was moving in its emotional intensity and poignancy. Despite dying at the age of only 44, Billie Holiday helped define the jazz era and her recordings are still widely sold today.

Shirley Chisholm (1924 – 2005): The first black Congresswoman. She was elected to the House of Representatives for NY in 1968. She used her time in Congress to campaign for women's and civil rights. She served from 1968 to 1983 and was the first black women to run for the Democratic Presidential nomination.

Coretta Scott King (1927 – 2006): Scott King was an author, musician, civil rights activist and wife of Martin Luther King. She played a prominent role in the civil rights campaigns, both before and after her husband's assassination. She founded the King Centre and campaigned for Martin Luther King Day to be a national holiday (established 1982)

Ellen Johnson Sirleaf (1938 –): Africa's first elected female Head of State. She served as president of Liberia from 2006 to 2018. She was jointly awarded the Nobel Peace Prize in 2011 for her work in supporting democracy and women's rights.

Oprah Winfrey (1954 –): Influential US media personality with groundbreaking chat show and own book club. Winfrey is active in many liberal causes and promotion of civil rights.

Wangari Muta Maathai (1940 – 2011): Kenyan environmental and political activist. Awarded the Nobel peace prize

2004 for *"her contribution to sustainable development, democracy and peace."*

Maya Angelou (1928 – 2014): American poet, writer and civil rights campaigner. Her autobiography *I Know Why the Caged Bird Sings* (1969) was received to wide-acclaim, she redefined the genre of autobiography to promote a different perspective on Africa-Americans.

Whoopi Goldberg (1955 –): American actress, comedian, author, and television host. Goldberg was the second black female actor to be awarded an Oscar for best-supporting actress. She was also awarded an Emmy Award (tv) a Grammy Award (music industry) and a Tony Award (live theatre)

Jackie Joyner-Kersee (1962-): One of the most successful female track and field athletes. Won Olympic gold in Heptathlon and Long Jump.

Michelle Obama (1964 –): Lawyer and writer, Michelle was the First Lady of the US during her husband's presidency 2009-17. She has often given well-received speeches at the Democratic convention. She is widely admired for the promotion of causes such as good health, exercise and nutrition — an approach that has transcended partisan boundaries.

Deratu Tulu (1972 –): The first Ethiopian female athlete to win Olympic gold. Tulu won gold at the 1992 Barcelona Olympics in the 10,000 m.

Tegla Laroupe (1973 –): A Keynan long distance runner and global spokesperson for peace. Broke world records from 20 km to the marathon. Now runs Tegla Loroupe Peace Foundation.

Nipsey Hussle (1985-2019): Born Ermias Joseph Asghedom (Eritrean/Black descent), was an American activist, entrepreneur, and Grammy Award winning rapper. Hussle focused on "giving solutions and inspiration" to young Black men like himself, motivating the Black community through his music, influence and community work, while speaking openly about his experiences with gang culture.

Serena Williams (1981 –): 23 single grand slam titles, 15 doubles titles. Also has won four Olympic gold medals. Williams is most decorated and highest earning female tennis player in history.

Kobe Bryant (1978-2020): Five N.B.A titles and one of the marquee players in the Los Angeles Lakers franchise. In 2015 Bryant wrote the poem "Dear Basketball," which won an Academy Award for best animated short film. A vocal advocate for the homeless Bryant and his wife, Vanessa started the Kobe and Vanessa Bryant Family Foundation aimed to reduce the number of homeless in Los Angeles.

Michael Jackson (1958 – 2009): A legend, a musician and a singer. Famous for albums such as 'Bad' and "Off the Wall". Jackson was also a pioneer of music videos.

Beyonce (1981 –): American singer, songwriter, record producer and actress. One of the best selling artists of the modern era. Also noted for positions on women and civil rights.

So What Is Black excellence?

Every single one of these Black leaders featured above have a distinct story and legacy. They all share some commonalities, poise and confidence that added to their iconic statuses. Dig a little deeper and you will uncover how they persevered and rose to greatness even through oppression and a biased government system. There, you'll find the link that bridges these Black pioneers together.

In short, Black excellence is more than a catchy hashtag or words written across the front of a sweatshirt. Black excellence is, in fact, our ancestor's wildest dreams come true. It's what we as people of African descent strive for each and every day. It's the livelihood of what keeps us going when it seems our humanity is being questioned. Black excellence is me and every other Black person working towards the advancement of our people. Together, and with the help of those that support Black excellence, we as a nation can continue to contribute and celebrate excellence in the Black community for generations to come.

REPARATIONS

$\mathcal{R}$eparation is the process of making amends for a wrong one has committed by paying money to those who have been wronged. This process is not foreign to the United States. Native Americans and Japanese Americans received reparations from the US government. Native Americans received land and billions of dollars for various benefits and programs for being forcibly exiled from their native lands. The Japanese Americans received $1.5 billion worth of reparation to those imprisoned during World War II. The United States, via the Marshall Plan, helped to ensure that Jews received reparations for the Holocaust, including making numerous investments over time. And in 1952, West Germany agreed to pay 3.45 billion Deutsche Marks to Holocaust survivors.

While slavery afforded some White families the ability to accrue tremendous wealth till this very day, Black Americans are the only group that has yet to receive reparations for state-sanctioned racial discrimination. Not a single penny has been paid to Black Americans for reparations.

The case for reparations can be made on economic, social, and moral grounds. The United States had multiple opportunities to compensate for slavery. Yet, nothing has been done. The US has missed every opportunity to make the American Dream a reality for all. Today, the US has yet to undertake any significant action to correct this disparity. Let's not forget, American slavery was brutal and detrimental to the success and freedom for future generations.

The American Dream Does Not Apply To All

The idea of living the American Dream is every US citizens ultimate goal. It's why millions of people world wide risk their lives to cross into the US. There's an underlying assumption that we all have an equal opportunity to generate the kind of life that brings meaning to the words penned in the Declaration of Independence (life, liberty and the pursuit of happiness). These words don't apply to all. Matter of fact, the Declaration of Independence was written by individuals who owned slaves. According to researchers, 41 of the 56 individuals who signed the Declaration of independence, owned slaves. The American dream states that with hard work, a person can own a home, start a business, and grow a nest egg for future generations to come. This belief, has been defied repeatedly by the United States government's own decrees that denied wealth building opportunities to Black Americans.

Today, the average White family has roughly 10 times the

amount of wealth as the average Black family. 10 times! In todays world, wealth disparity between races should be non existent. Yet, it still continues to wreak havoc in the progression of Black people today. White college graduates have over seven times more wealth than Black college graduates. Making the American Dream an equitable reality demands the same US government that denied wealth to Black American, to finally restore that deferred wealth through reparations to their descendants in the form of individual cash payments in the amount that will close the Black-White racial wealth gap. Reparations should come in the form of wealth building opportunities that address racial disparities in education, housing, and business ownership.

According to studies, over 3 billion dollars was the value assigned to the physical bodies of enslaved Black Americans to be used as free labor and production. In 1861, the value placed on cotton produced by slaves was estimated at $250 million. Without a doubt, slavery drastically enriched White slave owners and their descendants for generations. It fueled the country's economy while suppressing wealth building for the enslaved captives.

The Time Is Now!

The United States has yet to compensate descendants of enslaved Black Americans for their labor. Nor has the federal government make amends for the lost equity from anti-Black housing, transportation and business policy.

Slavery, Jim Crow segregation, anti-Black practices like redlining, and other discriminatory public policies in criminal justice and education have robbed Black Americans of the opportunities to build generational wealth.

This "bootstrapping" mentality that is often thrown around is not going to erase racial wealth disparities in the US. Black people alone cannot close the racial wealth gap by changing their individual behavior. Moreover, the racial wealth gap did not result from a lack of labor. Rather, it came from a lack of financial capital.

Not only does racial wealth disparities reveal inconsistencies in the American Dream. The financial and social consequences are significant and wide ranging. For instance, wealth is correlated with better health, educational, and economic outcomes. Furthermore, assets from homes, stocks, bonds, and retirement savings provide a financial safety net for the inevitable and avoidable curveballs life and the economy throws throughout a person's lifespan.

Recessions impact everyone, but wealth is distributed quite unevenly in the US. The inadequacy of a government sponsored safety net was made apparent in the wake of economic disasters like the 2008 housing crisis and natural ones like Hurricane Katrina in 2005. Those who can draw upon the equity in a home, savings, and securities are able to recover faster after economic downturns than those without wealth. As a result, millions of Black people were left homeless and displaced all over the country.

The lack of a social safety net and the racial wealth divide are currently on display amid the COVID-19 crisis. Disparities in access to health care along with inequities in economic policies combine to make Black people more vulnerable to negative consequences than White individuals. The United

States had numerous opportunities to amend for the racial wealth gap between White and Black Americans but failed to do so on numerous accounts.

Missed Opportunities To Amend For Slavery With Reparations

40 Acres and a Mule: The first major opportunity that the United States had and where it should have made amends for slavery was right after the Civil War. Union leaders including General William Sherman concluded that each Black family should receive 40 acres. Sherman signed Field Order 15 and allocated 400,000 acres of confiscated Confederate land to Black families. Some families were to receive mules left over from the war, (hence 40 acres and a mule).

However, after President Abraham Lincoln's assassination, President Andrew Johnson reversed Field Order 15 and returned land back to former slave owners. Instead of giving Blacks the means to support themselves, the federal government empowered former enslavers.

For example, in Washington DC, slave owners were paid reparations for lost property, (the freed slaves they owned). This practice was also common in nearby states. Many Black Americans with limited work options returned as sharecroppers to work on the same land for the very slave owners to whom they were once enslaved. Slave owners not only made money off the enslavement of Black Americans, but they also made money ten fold off the land that the formerly enslaved had no choice but to tend to.

The New Deal

There's never a bad time to do what's morally right, but the United States has had numerous opportunities to amend for slavery. In the 1930s, the United States was reeling from the 1929 stock market crash and was firmly engulfed in the Great Depression. The Franklin Roosevelt administration implemented a series of policies as part of his New Deal legislation, estimated to cost roughly $50 billion then, to catapult the country out of depression. Current estimates price the New Deal at about $50 trillion.

Two particular policies of the New Deal fell short in redressing American's racial wrongs—the GI Bill and Social Security. Though White and Black Americans fought in WWII, Black veterans were not allowed to redeem their postwar benefits like their White peers.

While the G.I Bill was mandated federally, it was implemented locally. The presence of racial housing covenants and redlining among local municipalities prohibited Blacks from utilizing federal benefits. White soldiers were afforded the opportunity to build wealth by sending themselves and their children to college and buy obtaining housing and small business grants.

Regarding Social Security, two key professions that would've improved equity in America were excluded from the legislation-domestic and farm workers. These omissions effectively excluded 60 percent of Black people across the US, and 75 percent in southern states who worked in these occupations. Roosevelt bargained these exclusionary provisions in the legislation on the backs of Black veterans and workers in order to propel mostly White America out of the Great Depression.

There are other policies and practices that contributed to racial wealth gap. Government sanctioned discrimination related to the 1862 Homestead Act, redlining, restrictive covenants, and convict leasing blocked Black people from the ability to gain wealth at similar rates as Whites. Separate from slavery, damages in monetary compensations should be awarded to Black people who were harmed by these policies and practices.

Reparations For Slavery And Anti-Black Policies

We know the monetary value that was placed on enslaved Blacks and the productivity of their labor, as well as the amount of the racial wealth gap. We've seen other groups receive restitutions while the federal government pulled back reparations for Black Americans.

Accordingly, if we want to close the racial wealth gap and live up to our moral creed to protect "life, liberty and the pursuit of happiness," a federal reparations package for Black Americans should be put in place. This package should include individual and collective public benefits that simultaneously builds wealth and eliminates debt among Black citizens.

It should be similar to the Harriet Tubman Community Investment Act, which was recently heard before the Maryland General Assembly where Ray testified on its behalf. The Harriet Tubman Community Investment Act aims to amend for slavery and its legacy by addressing education, homeownership, and business ownership barriers.

Individual Payments For Descendants Of Enslaved Black Americans

The US government owes lost wages as well as damages to the people it helped enslave. In addition to the lost wages, the accumulative amount of restitution for individuals should eliminate the racial wealth gap that currently exists. According to the Federal Reserve's most recent numbers in 2016, based on the Survey of Consumer Finances, White families had the highest median family wealth at $171,000, compared to Black and Hispanic families, which had a merely $17,600 and $20,700, respectively.

Free College Tuition To 4-Year Or 2-Year Colleges And Universities For Descendants Of Enslaved Black Americans

Black people should be able to use the tuition remission to obtain a bachelor's degree or an associate's/vocational or technical degree in order to further their education. Tuition should be available for public or private universities for Black college students. Considering the racial gap in the ability to obtain degrees at private schools, this part of the package will further help to reduce racial disparities by affording more social network access and opportunity structures.

Student Loan Forgiveness For Descendants Of Enslaved Black Americans

Student loan debt continues to be a significant barrier to wealth creation for Black college graduates. Among 25-55 year olds, about 40 percent of Black students compared to 30 percent of White students have student loan debt. Black college students have nearly $45,000 of student loan debt compared to about $30,000 for White college students.

Recent research finds that Black people are more likely to be subjected to unsubsidized loans. Furthermore, graduates of Historically Black Colleges (H.B.C) and Universities, compared to Predominately White Institutions, are more likely to receive subprime loans with higher interest rates.

Universities including Georgetown and Princeton are aiming to amend for the fact that the sale of slaves helped to fortify their university and establish them as an elite institutions of higher education on a global scale. Descendants of the slaves sold by Georgetown and Princeton are now entitled to full rights and benefits bestowed by those universities to obtain degrees across the higher education pipeline. Other universities, along with the federal government, should follow suit!

Down Payment Grants And Housing Grants For Descendants Of Enslaved Black Americans

Down payment grants will provide Black Americans with some initial equity in their homes relative to mortgage insurance loans. Housing revitalization grants will help Black

Americans to refurbish existing homes in neighborhoods that have been neglected due to a lack of government and corporate investments in predominately Black communities. Given recent settlements for predatory lending, low and fixed interest rates as well as property tax caps in areas in which housing prices are significantly devalued should be part of the package. According to Brookings research, after accounting for factors such as housing quality, neighborhood quality, education, and crime, owner-occupied homes in Black neighborhoods are undervalued by $48,000 per home on average, amounting to a whopping $156 billion that homeowners would have received if their homes were priced at market rates.

As gentrification continues to persist today, Black people are priced out of neighborhoods they helped to maintain. While the historical and current remnants of redlining and restrictive covenants inhibited investments, numerous Black Americans are being forced from their family because of tax increases as neighborhoods are being gentrified.

This is an important point because Democratic presidential candidates aimed to redress the racial wealth gap by focusing on historically redlined districts. Perry's research shows that these policies fall short of capturing a large segment of Black Americans.

Business Grants For Black Owned Businesses

Black owned businesses are more likely to be located in predominately Black neighborhoods that lack the infrastructure and businesses. Black business owners are less likely to obtain capital from banks to make their businesses successful. This reparations package for Black Americans is about restoring the wealth that has been extracted from Black people and communities. Reparations are all for nothing without enforcement of anti-discrimination policies that remove barriers to economic mobility and wealth building.

The architecture of the economy must change in order to create an equitable society for Black Americans. The racial wealth gap was created by prejudice policies which still persist till this very day. Federal intervention is needed to eradicate these polices and those who support them. In some respects, the question of who should receive reparations is more controversial than what or how much people should be awarded.

Who Should Receive Reparations?

One key question after deciding what a reparations package should include is who should qualify. In a perfect world, all Black people should receive reparations. As we all know, the world is far from perfect. In theory, anyone that can trace their heritage to people enslaved in US states and territories should be eligible for financial compensation for slavery.

Black people who can show how they were excluded from various policies after emancipation should seek separate damages too. For instance, a person like Senator Cory Booker whose parents are descendants of slaves would qualify for slavery reparations whereas Vice President Kamala Harris (Jamaican immigrant father and Indian immigrant mother) and President Barack Obama (Kenyan immigrant father and white mother) may seek redress for housing and/or education segregation. On the other hand, Sasha and Malia Obama (whose mother is Michelle Obama, a descendant of enslaved Africans) would qualify for reparations.

To determine qualification, birth records can initially be used to verify if a person was classified as Black American. Economist Sandy Darity, asserts that people should show a consistent pattern of identification. Census records can then be used to determine if a person has consistently identified as Black American. Lastly, a DNA testing can be used to determine lineage. This is how Senator Booker, who first introduced a reparations bill in the Senate, discovered that his ancestors stemmed from Sierra Leone.

Paid In Full

For the descendants of the 12.5 million Africans who were shipped in chains from Western Africa, "America has a genetic birth defect when it comes to the question of race," as stated recently by US Representative Hakeem Jeffries. If America is to amend for this defect, reparations for Black Americans is part of the healing and reconciliation process.

When the architects of our republic wrote the magnificent words of the Constitution and the Declaration of Independence, they were signing a promissory note to which every American was to fall heir. It's obvious that America has defaulted on this promissory note as her citizens of color are overlooked and undervalued. Instead of honoring this sacred obligation, America has given Black Americans a check marked "insufficient funds". But we refuse to believe that the bank of justice is bankrupt.

Given the lingering legacy of slavery on the racial wealth gap, the monetary value we know that was placed on enslaved Blacks, the fact that other groups have received reparations, and the fact that Black people were originally awarded reparations only to have them rescinded; means that it's finally time to make amends to the descendants of enslaved Black Americans. As we think about our political future, this part of history lives on. In the meantime, will the ideals of the revolution of freedom, equality, and justice, be for all Americans? Can we as a nation break the wealth gap between White and Black Americans? Who knows, only time will tell.